THANK GOD FOR
WHAT YOU HAVE

TRUST GOD FOR WHAT YOU NEED

CHANGING THE WORLD ONE PERSON AT A TIME

CYRIS J. JONES

Follow Cyris J. Jones

Social Media Outlets:

Facebook: @cyrisjones
Instagram: @Cyris Jones
Email: cyris@cyrisjones.com
Website: https://cyrisjones.com

CONTENTS

DEDICATION

This book is dedicated to the people in the world who have somehow forgotten about the goodness of God in their lives. For those who are trusting God to deliver them from something, get them to their next destination, or renew a right spirit in their lives. My parents' examples of Godly love, compassion, kindness, and perseverance have shaped my life and the lives of so many who know them. They have taught me so much and have been an inspiration throughout my life. I wanted this book to help others around the world remember that we serve a God of hope, compassion, forgiveness, love, and abundance.

This book should serve as a compelling reminder that God's love conquers all difficulties, overcomes all obstacles, and will always bring the possible to the impossible situations in life.

This book should serve as an inspiring testament to the transformative power of God's grace and mercy in all of our lives.

FOREWORD

Cyris Jones has written a powerful book, "Thank God for What You Have, Trust God for What You Need," that resonated deeply with me. His message reminds me of my core belief: "You don't have to be great to get started, but you must get started to be great." This book speaks to the importance of appreciating what we have while trusting in God's plan for the future.

When I first came across Cyris Jones, I was struck not only by his passion but by his deep conviction to inspire others to live with faith, gratitude, and purpose. Reading Cyris' words, I was reminded of Dr. Myles Munroe's profound insight that "the greatest tragedy in life is not death, but a life without purpose,' Cyris helps readers discover that purpose by inspiring them to recognize their blessings and step forward in faith.

In a world filled with uncertainty, Cyris reminds us of timeless principles that have anchored lives for generations: the importance of trusting in God's plan and being thankful for what we already have. In "Thank God for What You Have, Trust God for What You Need," Cyris shares his journey with authenticity and vulnerability. He reminds us that even in the face of adversity, we can find strength by shifting our perspective from lack to gratitude. This shift is not only powerful but transformational. As someone who has dedicated my life to helping people unlock their potential, I see the value in the wisdom Cyris offers in this book.

Life will throw challenges our way, but Cyris shows us how to navigate those storms with faith as our guide. Through his words, we are reminded that our greatest power comes from aligning our hearts with divine purpose and trusting that everything we need will come in due time.

Whether you're at the beginning of your journey or have been walking with faith for years, this book will uplift you, challenge you, and most importantly, remind you of the abundance that is already within your grasp. It's more than just a book – it's a call to live a life of faith, commitment, and gratitude.

I have always believed that 'most people fail in life not because they aim too high and miss, but because they aim too low and hit,' and this book challenges us to aim higher, trust more, and embrace greatness.

This book will forever change your life. Cyris is serious about changing the world, one person at a time. I encourage you to read it, recommend it to your friends, family, co-workers and church members.

Cyris is a rising voice in inspirational literature, and I believe his work has the potential to change lives. I am honored to lend my voice to this work, and I know that Cyris' message will resonate deeply with you, just as it did with me. This is a book that I highly recommend.

Yours in GREATNESS,
Les Brown
Speaker, Author, Trainer

ACKNOWLEDGEMENT

This book would not have been possible without the grace and mercy of God in my life and the help and support of my family, friends, and co-workers.

To my wonderful wife Terri and my amazing children Christian and Torri; thank you for your patience and your unique critique providing transparent feedback on my work. Your understanding of my purpose and passion for writing this book helped guide my determination to never give up.

A special thanks to my wonderful parents Madis and Willie Jones for the many years of selflessness, kindness, and perseverance that were so instrumental in shaping my life, as well as the lives of my siblings and so many others.

A special thanks to my little brother Michael Jones who demonstrated resilience and perseverance throughout his life. His ability to bring our family together has been a testament of compassion, Godly love, and kindness and has served as a guiding light that enabled me to write this and many other books.

A special thanks to my maternal and paternal grandparents for being such great role models in my life.

Special thanks to Dr. Denise Nicholson, my mentor, my friend, my writing coach, accountability partner, the owner of the Writing Incubator Program, and CEO of Bold Publishing Company. Dr. Denise a sincere thank you for your patience, dedication, and professionalism during this process. Your commitment to helping so many of us in the writing incubator challenge to transfer our words from our heads to paper is so amazing and appreciated. I appreciate you and your relentless passion in guiding each of us to book writing excellence.

Special thanks to my mentor and motivational speaking coach, Les Brown, who has been named one of the top five speakers in the world. Les Brown, thank you for your undying passion and commitment to your craft. You are so determined to help us all to bring out the greatness that is within us and to use our stories as a testimony to help change so many lives across the world.

Special thanks to Mrs. Shirley Brown Danzy, author of, "The Power to Succeed", for introducing me to the writing process and this community of literary excellence. Thank you for believing in me before I was able to believe in myself in the writing journey.

INTRODUCTION

"Today is a new day, you can start fresh by wiping the slate clean. Begin again! Today you can embrace kindness, work for the common good, practice compassion and stand up for justice. Listen with your whole heart, offer hope and love, aspire for more, make a difference and be the change that you wish to see in the world." - **Marla Rae**

Early morning, during my daily devotion, I thank God for all that he has done in my life. I reflect on the grace and mercy that he has shown my family each day. My mind often wonders where I would be without God in my life. *Where would my life have taken me if I hadn't chosen God as my Lord and Savior?*

When I hear people complaining about their families and their life situations, I seldomly hear them sounding optimistic or even giving thanks to God for what they already have. I often see that the people complaining are the same ones who have a job, a car, a home; they usually have a family and are walking and talking freely without limitations or constraints.

Everyone yearns for more of what they have or what they see others having. It is important that you do not take your daily blessings for granted. God is a God of praise and worship. "Stay humble so that you will not have to be humbled." - **Steve Maraboli**

This book is meant to serve as a reminder to the world that God is relentless in His love and devotion to us all. He wants us to be the guiding light in the lives of people that are in despair or that have lost sight of their purpose in life. He wants us to never give up hope in any situation that seems hopeless. He will never leave you, nor forsake you.

Give him the praise and the glory for what he has done, is doing and will do in your life. Faith is having the "Courage and Discipline" to believe that God will deliver to you that which He has promised you. Trust God's timing, even when you cannot see his hand or understand his plan.

As a young boy growing up in Central Mississippi in the late 1970's and early 80's, I can remember working in my parents' and my grandparents' fields. One summer day while I was picking cucumbers, the "Holy Spirit" came into my life. God touched my heart and mind in a way that I had never been touched before. With tears streaming down my face crying uncontrollably, I gave my life to Christ, right then and there.

Even though I had already been baptized and had been raised in the church, I had never truly felt the Holy Spirit in my life until that moment. For me, that was the beginning of understanding God's will for my life and how he wanted me to change the world, one person at a time. After that day I could talk to God, I could hear his voice, and see the manifestations that he had for my life and for my family.

I knew that God had a plan for my life; I understood that regardless of what I did going forward, I would need to re-align my thinking towards achieving God's plan for my life and not my earthly selfish plans. Making God the top priority in my life shaped my future. I had a sense of purpose that would always lead me and guide me in the right direction. I knew that I had an inner conviction that would not rest until I did what was right and just.

Over time I have realized that everyday would not be a bed of roses nor a sunshiny day. I know that on my path to glory I will encounter some thorns and stormy days, but I know that God is protecting me and preparing me for greatness.

I know that he will never send me on a journey without providing for my daily needs. I realized that just because you cannot see it does not mean that God does not already have your blessing on the way. Always give thanks for what you see and for what you cannot see. Just have faith and know that your Blessing has your name on it and that it is on the way. Always remember that while you are waiting for your blessing, why not be a blessing to someone else.

In my daily walk of life, inspirational gospel music has helped me to focus on praising God. Inspirational gospel music excites my soul, inspires my confidence and strengthens my faith in God. It helps me to understand that when prayers and praises go up that blessings and favor come down.

This inspiration comes from Psalms 149:1-5 "Praise ye the Lord, Sing unto the Lord a new song, and his praise in the congregation of saints. Let the saints be joyful in glory: let them sing aloud upon their bed."

"When you have no strength, lean on God and you will become powerful." – **Dwight L. Moody.**

UNCONDITIONAL LOVE

When love is demonstrated as sacrifice, compassion, and humanity to others, it can forever transform lives.

Most people consider love as an action word. It shows an act or a kind gesture. Just saying that you love someone is not as effective as demonstrating the act of loving someone. Everyone wants to genuinely feel loved and valued. The Bible says that "Love conquers all things, bears all things, hopes all things and endures all things."- (1 Corinthians 13:7) This helps us to understand that nothing of great substance will come easily. We will often have to pass through numerous difficulties and hardships on our earthly journey, but God gives us the gift of unconditional love to see us through.

Unconditional Love is often referred to as a type of love that is not contingent on any conditions or requirements. It is love that is given freely, without expecting anything in return. Unconditional Love is selfless, forgiving, enduring and everlasting. It transcends any limitations or boundaries.

John 3:16 - " For God so loved the world that He gave His only begotten Son, that whosoever believes in Him should not perish but have everlasting life."

God provided the ultimate example of unconditional love by allowing Jesus to die on the cross to free us from sin. All power was in His hands to intervene and bring His son home but he did not because he loves us so much. Jesus showed us that sacrifice and pain are a part of fulfilling God's will for our lives. God's message that eternal salvation outweighs short term pain and suffering should resonate in our hearts and minds every day.

I am reminded daily of God's amazing sacrifice and his love for the world. I often think about how Jesus showed compassion so many times in the Bible. Throughout His earthly ministry, Jesus demonstrated His unconditional love for others by blessing and serving the poor, the sick and the distressed. He told His disciples, "This is my commandment, that ye love one another, as I have loved you." (John 15:12)

I often look back over my life and I see how God worked through my parents, teaching them how to show unconditional love throughout my life. I look at these acts of unconditional love and reflect on how each instance methodically shaped my perception of love and its impact on the lives of others. Their selfless acts taught me how to live a life as a servant and giver of my time, finances and talents.

When I was around 4 years of age, I remember my little brother who was around 2 ½ years old suffering a tragic accident. Previously he had suffered a brain injury from a fall while trying to walk when he was around 10 months old.

Fast forward less than 2 years later, he was severely burned by hot ashes from a fireplace in our home. While my dad was asleep in the bed and my mom was preparing breakfast, my brother began playing near the fireplace. He accidentally fell in.

My parents immediately raced him to the hospital. My dad drove frantically at speeds over ninety miles an hour to the hospital. When they reached the burn center the doctors worked tirelessly to stabilize his condition. My brother suffered 1st, 2nd and 3rd degree burns on his face and hands. Over a series of weeks and months they performed several skin graphs and reconstructive surgeries.

I could only imagine my brother's pain and suffering as he went through this traumatic event in his life. I also reflect on the pain and suffering that my parents endured as well. They would forever ask themselves what could have been done to prevent the tragedy, what actions could we have taken to ease his pain?

The answer was painfully simple: nothing. My brother's accident, although devastating, was the beginning of acts of unconditional love, humility, and compassion. Unfortunately, and fortunately, this was divine intervention.

My parents grew closer to one another, to our family and most importantly closer to God. They were thankful that my little brother had not died due to his injuries. They were even more committed to taking care of his special needs.

They knew that their lives would forever change because of this event. My mom gave up her career in pre-school teaching and focused her efforts on the care of my little brother. My dad focused on being the single breadwinner for a family of thirteen and taking care of his aging parents as well as the special care of my little brother.

They knew that the road ahead would be long and difficult, but they were committed to thanking God and trusting his word. 1

Corinthians 10:13 can be translated as "God is faithful and He will never give you more than you can handle."

Growing up, not going to church was never an option. Oh yes, you were going regardless. My parents and grandparents were always active members of our local church. In fact, my siblings and I were one-third of the children's choir. In retrospect that was the beginning of my love and passion for gospel music. While my mom was a member of the Senior choir, my dad left the musical endeavors to my mom. He figured one singing sensation was enough.

I remember both parents getting on their knees and praying every single night before bed and constantly reading and studying their Bibles. As children, we were required to learn the Lord's prayer and other Bible verses. This was my early introduction to having a daily devotion and spending time with God.

Max Lucado - (I Choose Love) - "No occasion justifies hatred; no injustice warrants bitterness. I choose love. Today I will love God and what God loves."

Our parents taught us to be respectful to everyone and to always be honest. We were taught to love and respect everyone regardless of age, race, gender, etc. Our parents made each of us feel loved and cherished. My dad taught us to always work hard and to always put in an honest day's work for an honest day's pay. He taught us to put God first in all that we do and to always give God the praise and glory.

My mom was the glue that kept everything together. She made sure that we were active in sports and always gave our best efforts. She taught us to be humble and thankful. She taught us to always have a selfless and positive attitude and to always have faith in God.

Growing up, our parent's home was a haven for children throughout our community. Parents felt safe allowing their children to travel to our home for weekly sporting events like friendly games of football, soccer, baseball, and softball. Our parents made sure that everyone was treated with love and respect. Often my parents would participate in the sporting events with my little brother as well. This was helpful in relieving stress from the multitude of tasks required to take care of my little brother's special needs.

Proverbs 22:6 says, "Train up a child in the way he should go, and when he is old, he will not depart from it."

So many times, I watched my parents sow seeds of love and hope into the lives of other children and adults in our community. Their examples of love and compassion resonated in my heart and mind. Our parents showed my siblings and I the true meaning of love each day. We may not have had everything that we wanted but we always had everything that we needed.

Even though we did not always wear the latest fashion or name brand clothing, our parents always made sure that each of us were well dressed wherever we went.

Growing up, school was a top priority for us. Our parents constantly made sure that we all focused on our education and stressed the importance of getting a quality education.

One summer afternoon I remember traveling with my dad to pick my mom up from choir practice at our church. While we were waiting my dad explained to me that he wanted each of his children to put forward their best efforts. He would often say, "I want you to be better than me. I know that you can do it. Always put God first in your life."

He told me how much he loved me and to always take care of my little brother and my mom. At the time I was surprised to see my dad showing so many emotions, but it really meant a lot to me. It was forever etched in my mind.

I learned from my mom and dad that family was important, but most importantly your relationship with God should be your #1 priority in your life.

Max Lucado -

"Love, Joy, peace, patience, kindness, goodness, faithfulness, gentleness and self control. To those I commit my day. If I succeed, I will give thanks"

"If I fail, I will seek grace. And then when the day is done, I will place my head on my pillow and rest."

I read the following:

Ten Steps to Loving Unconditionally

"Choose to Love Unconditionally"

"Let Go of Expectations"

"Accept the Other Person"

"Drop the Judgements"

"Speak Your Loved One's Love Language"

"Forgive Others"

"Love Yourself"

"Practice"

"Be committed"

"Seek God"

<u>10 Ways to Love</u>

Listen without interrupting.
Share without pretending.
Speak without accusing.
Enjoy without complaint.
Give without sparing.
Trust without wavering.
Pray without ceasing.
Forgive without punishing.
Answer without arguing.
Promising without forgiving.

Conditional Love	vs	Unconditional Love
Selfish		Selfless
Rooted in Ego		Rooted in Soul
Seeks Control		Seeks Freedom
Has expectations		No expectations
Judgemental		Non - judgemental
Looks for another to complete them		Is already whole and complete
Feels threatened		Doesn't worry
Needy		Needs nothing
Jealous		Secure with self

Jake Woodard - Author

Chapter One - Key Takeaways

1) God showed the greatest example of sacrifice to the world.

2) Jesus showed his greatest love to the world.

3) Love is patient and love is kind.

4) Always turn tragedy into triumph.

5) Parents should always love their children unconditionally with acts of compassion, sacrifice, and kindness. Always plant seeds of greatness and watch them grow. Be the example that God wants you to be.

"The best things that you can give children, next to good habits, are good memories." - **Sydney Harris**

Motivational Songs:

1) "Believe For It" - CeCe Winans

2) "Psalms 42" - Tori Kelly

3) "The Goodness of God" – CeCe Winans

4) "What A Beautiful Name" - Hillsong United

Scripture References:

1) John 3:16

2) 1 John 4:7-9

3) 1 Corinthians 13:13

4) Proverbs 3:3

Motivational Quote -

"Remember, you are not alone in the awesome responsibility of leading your family. I go ahead of you on your journey of life. I search out your options and show you the way that you should go. In difficult places of life, I carry you as a father carries his son. I faithfully guide you all the way! The key to success is trusting me and teaching your children by your example the importance of following me wholeheartedly."

Love,
The Lord Your God,
Who Goes Before You

-LeAnn Weiss (Deuteronomy 1:30-36)

A Prayer For "Unconditional Love"

"Dear Heavenly Father"

I come before you with a humble and grateful heart, seeking Your presence and Your unconditional love for my life. Your love knows no boundaries, no limits, and no conditions. Your love is pure, steadfast, and everlasting. Thank You God for loving me despite my many flaws and imperfections.

Lord, please help me to grasp the depth of Your unconditional love more and more each day. Let Your love transform me from within, so that I may reflect Your love to others. Teach me to love others as You have loved me, without expecting anything in return, freely and unreservedly.

Lord please grant me strength to forgive others as You have forgiven me, and to extend grace and mercy to those who may not deserve it, just as You have extended Your grace and mercy unto me. Lord please help me to see others through Your eyes, with sincere compassion and empathy.

Father God, in times of doubt or fear, please remind me of Your unwavering love that never fails. May Your love be the anchor that steadies me in the storms of life and the guiding light that leads me on the path of righteousness.

Thank You Lord, for Your unconditional love that surpasses all my understanding. May it fill my heart and overflow into every area of my life. Lord, I surrender myself wholeheartedly to You, trusting in Your perfect love.

In the precious name of Jesus - Amen

CHAPTER NOTES

_____

_____

_____

_____

_____

_____

_____

_____

_____

_____

_____

_____

_____

_____

_____

_____

_____

_____

_____

_____

_____

_____

_____

_____

GET IN AGREEMENT WITH GOD

Understanding God's will and plan for your life
is critical in your daily walk with God.

"Getting in agreement with God" means aligning your thoughts, beliefs, and actions with what you understand to be God's will or direction for your path forward in life. Often this involves studying various scriptures in the Bible, prayer, reflection, and striving to live in a way that reflects God's desires for humanity, such as showing love, compassion, and sacrifice towards others.

The level of commitment required to understand God's will for one's life may vary. It takes discipline and patience not only to hear from God but also to accept his will and plan for your life.

The book of Jonah, tells how Jonah initially disobeys God's command to go to the city of Nineveh and give prophecy, causing him to be swallowed up by the whale as punishment. However, Jonah prays to God for forgiveness, and God both spares his life and spares the city of Nineveh. This only happened after Jonah obeyed God's plan for his life after being given a second chance.

Sometimes people do not really want to hear God's plan for their life, simply because it is not what they want it to be. It may not be the glamorous path that one desires or it may be a difficult path or plan.

So often people ignore it and try to do it on their own or try to do it their own way. From personal experience, let me tell you that doing it your way vs God's way will have consequences. You will waste a lot of time, energy, and money trying to do your own thing, your own way.

So always keep calm, be patient, and listen with your whole heart. God may be whispering the direction for your life with a gentle voice. Are you listening?

Proverbs 3:5-7 says "Trust in the Lord with all your heart and lean not on your own understanding. In all thy ways acknowledge him and he shall direct thy paths."

I remember my transition from high school to college. It was an eye-opening experience. I was away from home for the first time in my life and I could do anything that I wanted. I could come home at any time, go anywhere that I wanted to and not have to answer to anyone. I would often go out to clubs and parties with my friends and roommates. I was living on the edge and having fun doing it. I stopped going to church on a consistent basis. I had my own job, my own money and I was living it up…in all the wrong ways. My grades were suffering. I went from getting all A's and one B in my first semester in school to nearly failing all my classes the second semester. I was not following the plan that God had laid out for me.

One night I was rushed to the ER for abdominal pain. I was in so much pain that I could barely walk. I wasn't sure what was going on, but I was so scared. I was later diagnosed with having a bowel obstruction. A part of my intestines had twisted and was causing pain and an obstruction.

Several years earlier around the age of 10 years old, I had an emergency appendectomy. My appendix ruptured on the operating table. Five days later I had to undergo another emergency surgery. Infection had set up inside my body, I had a severe fever, and I was in critical condition. The initial surgery location had to be re-opened. They had to quickly install drainage tubes in my side for the remaining infection to exit my body. I was able to bounce back from the surgeries, but I still had a lot of pain periodically due to internal scar tissue.

So, as I laid in the ER, my mind began to reflect on the day I accepted God into my life. As I mentioned earlier, I accepted God into my life while I was working in the fields of my parents farm. Now God was again reminding me of His plan for my life. He reminded me that life was precious and that I didn't have time to squander it away. He reminded me of my assignment.

He reminded me about the plans that he had for my life and the impact that I would have on my family, friends, and the rest of the world. I began to realize that the things that I promised God that I would do, I wasn't doing consistently. I had to find my way back to God; he never left me, but I somehow had abandoned him.

After leaving the hospital, I realized that I had to get it together, refocus and redirect my efforts. As my parents had told me so many times before, it was important to put God as the head of my life. I started going back to church on a regular basis. I located a church closer to college and made attending it a top priority.

I realized that I had to reprioritize my life:

First of all , I had to prioritize God as being most important in my life. I had to refocus on His plan for my life. I also had to seek the support and guidance of my family. Next, I had to rededicate my efforts in school, get serious about my career, and look to advance at work to secure my future.

Finally, I had to separate from friends that didn't have my best interest at heart.

In Psalms 32:8 The Lord says "I will guide you along the best path for your life. I will advise you and watch over you."

6 Ways to determine God's will and plan for your life.

- **Prayer and Meditation** – Regular communication with God through prayer and meditation can help foster a closer relationship. Have a daily time and location that you have dedicated to a daily devotional. Through these principles, God can provide guidance and direct clarity to your plans.

- **Study Religious Scriptures Daily** – Reading and studying scriptures can provide insight into the values and principles that should guide your life according to your faith. Scriptures often speak to your situation and can help you to understand God's desires and plans for your life.

- **Seek Guidance from Religious Leaders** – Conversations with pastors, associate ministers, priests, or other religious leaders can provide counsel and advice based on biblical teachings and wisdom.

- **Observe Doors Opening and Closing** – Sometimes God's guidance can be seen in the opportunities and obstacles that arise in your life. Doors that open effortlessly may be seen as signs of God's plan for your life. Alternately, closed doors may signify that it's not the path that God desires for your life.

- **Look for Gifts and Talents** – Identifying what you are good at and what brings you fulfillment and joy can be helpful in understanding God's plan. Using your talents and abilities in a way that allows you to feel fulfilled and serve others can be seen as alignment with God's intentional plans for your life.

- **Listen to your Inner Voice** – Oftentimes God can and will speak to you through your conscience or that "still small voice" inside **(The Holy Spirit)**. Paying attention and listening closely can be a way to determine direction from God.

  - Determining whether it is indeed God speaking to you involves ensuring that the message is consistent with the nature of God as described in the biblical teachings. It often requires patience, your ability and willingness to listen and the seeking of confirmation through your prayer and the counsel of others.

Chapter Two - Key Takeaways:

1) Always align your plans with God's plan for your life.

2) Pray and meditate daily to gain an understanding of God's plan and will for your life.

3) Listen with your heart and mind as the Holy Spirit directs your path to greatness.

4) Be patient and obedient to God's plan and will for your life.

5) When you find yourself off the prescribed path……. don't panic, get back in alignment with God's will and his plan for your life. You know when you are out of God's will!

Motivational Songs:

1) "Open My Heart" - Yolanda Adams

2) "Reckless Love" - Cory Asbury

3) "I Look to You" - Whitney Houston

4) "Bless The Lord" - Matt Maher

Scripture References:

1) Psalms 32:8

2) Proverbs 3:5-7

3) Mark 11:24

4) Matthew 19:26

Motivational Quote -

"Knowing is not enough; we must apply. Willing is not enough; we must do" - **Joann Wolfgang von Goethe**

A Prayer To "Get In Agreement With God"

"Dear Heavenly Father"

I come before You with a heart open to Your will and Your plan for my life. Help me, O Lord, to align my desires and ambitions with Your perfect plan. Grant me the wisdom and discernment to recognize Your voice amidst the noise of this world. Give me the strength to surrender my will to Yours, knowing that Your plans for me are good, pleasing, and perfect.

Forgive me for the times I have sought my own way instead of Yours. Teach me to trust in Your divine wisdom and timing, even when I cannot see the full picture. Help me to walk in faith, knowing that You are guiding every step I take.

May Your peace, which surpasses all understanding, guard my heart and mind in Christ Jesus. Lead me in paths of righteousness for Your name's sake, and may I bring glory to You in all that I do. Thank You for Your unfailing love and grace, and for Your promise to never leave nor forsake me.

In the precious name of Jesus - Amen

CHAPTER NOTES

CONQUERING THE STORM

Learning How to Turn Your Test into a Testimony for Others.
I will sing of the goodness of God.

As I began preparing to write this book, I had very meaningful dialogue with people like Dr. Denise Nicholson and legendary speaker Mr. Les Brown. I also spent time listening to motivational speakers like Myron Golden, Emily Ford, Natasha Graziano, Alex Rodriguez and others. I realized that people have gone through sexual abuse, physical abuse, mental abuse, personal loss, health issues and so much more.

I realized that so many people are suffering and are hurting inside and outside. I began to realize that acceptance and forgiveness are critical to the healing process. Sometimes it may seem as though it takes all of the strength that you can muster, but you have to forgive and move on with your life. Don't allow others to have power over your life. In many cases forgiveness helps you to heal. So many people are going through, have gone through, or will be going through so many types of storms in their lives.

A "storm" can be defined as a significant challenge, difficulty, or a period of turmoil that you might face in life. To conquer the storm implies not just surviving these challenges, but emerging stronger, wiser, or more resilient as a result of having gone through adversity.

In this chapter I would like to help strengthen your ability to prevail through your storms and adversities and turn your test into a testimony. I will provide biblical examples and solutions as well as practical examples and solutions throughout this chapter. Our God is a magnificent God. He has said in his words, "That he will never leave us nor forsake us."(Deuteronomy 31:6)

Life's storms come in many forms, each uniquely challenging and capable of leaving deep scars. Understanding these storms is the first step toward navigating them effectively and finding the path to healing.

The types of storms in life may vary in size and impact including but not limited to the following:

- **Personal Loss** - Experiencing the death of a loved one, the end of a significant relationship, the loss of a pet, etc. can feel like a storm due to the intense emotions and personal adjustments required.

- **Abuse** - Recovering from sexual abuse, mental abuse, physical abuse, etc. can and will always represent a storm of difficult proportions in one's life.

- **Financial Struggles** - Encountering a job loss, unexpected expenses, debt, or other financial crises can create a storm of worry and the need for substantial life adjustments.

- **Health Issues** - Facing a serious illness, injury, depression, low self-esteem, or mental health issues for either you or a family member can disrupt your daily life and create tremendous stress.

- **Battling Addictions** - Fighting through addictions, like alcohol addiction, illegal drug addictions, prescription drug addiction, self-harming addictions, tobacco addictions, food addictions, eating addictions, gambling addictions, shopping addictions, pornography addiction, sex addiction, etc. can cause stress in your life and the lives of your family members.

- **Work Related Stress** - Challenges at work such as workplace conflicts, high work demands, job insecurity, doing stressful project work, can all contribute to feelings of going through a storm.

- **Family or Family Conflict** - Disputes, misunderstandings, divorce or just tension in relationships with family members, friends, or partners can lead to emotional distress and turmoil in your life.

- **Life Transitions** - Major changes such as moving to a new location, new home, changing jobs, changing schools, or adjusting to a new phase of your life like (puberty, starting high school, starting college, retirement, or an empty nest) can feel destabilizing and very stressful.

Each of these examples represents a type of storm that requires coping mechanisms, support and sometimes professional help to navigate successfully. Later in this chapter we will discuss specific spiritual and practical coping strategies for each type of storm.

Always please understand that you are never alone. Your family, church members, pastors, friends and professional support are available.

Most importantly always remember that God is there and will always be there for you. Even in times that you can't see a way out, always press forward. In many cases God is working in front of you to remove roadblocks or obstacles, walking behind you to guide you and encourage you step by step, or in some cases he is even carrying you through your storm.

From a biblical perspective the story of Job personifies the power of God and the faith and endurance of Job while facing numerous tragedies in his life.

Job, a man of great faith and integrity, faced unimaginable trials that tested his resolve and belief in God. Job endured the loss of his wealth, children, and health, yet he remained steadfast in his belief and devotion to God.

In the midst of his storm, Job questioned why he, a righteous man in his own eyes, was suffering such profound loss and affliction. He questioned the fairness of God's actions and God's wisdom. He sought to understand why God would allow such intense trials and storms in his life. He struggled with understanding God's divine plan and the reasons behind his sufferings, but ultimately demonstrated his great faith in God and submitted to His supreme power and authority.

Despite the urging of his friends to curse God, abandon his faith and to give up, Job remained steadfast to his innocence and to his faith, declaring: "Though he slay me, yet will I hope in him" (Job 13:15).

His unwavering trust in God's goodness and justice sustained him through the darkest moments. In the end, God restored Job's fortunes twofold and blessed him with a new family. Job's story illustrates the power of faith and perseverance in the face of adversity. It teaches us that even in our deepest trials, trusting in God's plan and remaining faithful can lead to renewed strength and eventually full and abundant restoration. Job's example inspires us to hold fast to our faith, knowing that God's purposes are beyond our understanding and His faithfulness endures forever.

From a personal and practical standpoint, I often think back on my parents and how they managed through various storms during their 67 years of marriage. One significant storm was the loss of my younger brother. My parents worked selflessly for over 39 years to nurture and care for my brother. On the night of February 24th, 2012, my parents had just tucked my brother in bed for the night.

This date is significant because it's also my birthday. Around 1:00 a.m. on the morning of February 25th my dad went in to check on my brother like he normally would, and he didn't see him lying in his bed. As he frantically searched for him, he found his lifeless body on the side of the bed. He immediately yelled for my mom's assistance, and she quickly called 911 and later called for assistance from their neighbors.

I was immediately notified and quickly began my journey to my parents' home and then to the hospital. The hour-long drive was filled with phone calls trying frantically to get information on my brother's status and to alert my siblings of the situation.

When I arrived at the hospital, I was informed that my brother had passed. I immediately went to be by his side. I entered the room and was overwhelmed with grief as I saw his lifeless body lying on the table. I kissed him on the forehead and laid my head on his head. I told him how much he meant to me and how much I loved him.

I then turned my focus to comforting my parents. For over 39 years they had taken care of my brother and managed to make his life as comfortable as possible.

He would often have seizures and shake uncontrollably for a few seconds and required additional support to overcome each episode.

Unfortunately, this time he did not survive. I thanked my mom and dad for always being there for my brother and for their constant dedication to taking care of him. My mom and dad were devastated, and heartbroken. Their child was no longer with them. Whenever you saw one you would almost always see all three of them. They were inseparable. They were the 3 Musketeers so to speak. Their love for one another was priceless. For 39 years one of their main purposes in life was taking care of their family but primarily taking care of my brother's special needs.

Six months later as they were picking up the pieces of their lives, my dad fell sick. He had to have emergency surgery due to a bowel obstruction.

He made it through the surgery and was doing well. Four days later he was moved to a recovery stay unit and after spending the night began to show signs of sepsis. He was immediately rushed back to the hospital and was placed in the ICU. His condition worsened within a few hours. All my dad's major organs had begun to shut down.

The doctor informed my family that my dad's condition was critical and that the chance of him surviving through the night was very low. He asked us to notify the rest of the family and to prepare them for the worst.

But my mom was not having it. That message just went straight past her. After the doctor walked away, she immediately said, "Your dad may have to go on kidney dialysis after this." I immediately stopped and was at a loss for words. I said, "Mom, the doctor is saying that dad may not make it through the night." She replied, "He will be okay. He's going to make it through."

I remember comforting my mother but most importantly I remember her constantly thanking God. The Bible says, "to call those things that aren't, as though they are, until they come to be."- (Mark 11:23) And that was exactly what my mother was doing. She placed her trust in God, and this allowed me to trust God even more and to pray even harder.

I began to thank God even more and I knew that I had to trust Him for the miraculous healing power that was needed to save my dad's life.

Within minutes, I could hear the Holy Spirit whispering to me, "It's not his time." A sense of warmth and comfort came over my body. I felt assured that despite what the doctor said and despite the obvious circumstances, my dad was going to pull through. Throughout the night my dad lay in a medically induced coma. Throughout the next few days he remained in ICU, but slowly began to show signs of recovery.

Within four days he was awake, and the doctors were very optimistic that he would have a long and tough road to recovery but that he would survive. Over the next nine months, my dad remained in the hospital, extended stay recovery unit or nursing home as he recovered.

My family and I were relentless in staying with my dad daily and nightly. Someone stayed with him around the clock making sure that he was given the best possible care. My mom visited him every single day during his recovery. "Her faith never wavered."

My dad was eventually discharged and allowed to go home. He required daily professional assistance and was confined to a wheelchair but went on to live a productive life for the next eight years. My mom remained faithfully by his side as they enjoyed each other's love and affection each day. They both remained optimistic and thankful to

God for all that he had done throughout their journey. My dad passed away eight years later from Stage 4 lung cancer.

Finally, surviving a storm in your personal life involves a mixture of having a strong spiritual foundation, self-care, support systems, and practical strategies. It is also important to understand what phase of the storm process you are in.

1) You are entering a storm.

2) You are in the middle of a storm.

3) You are exiting a storm.

Combining spiritual and practical coping strategies to navigate life's storms can provide a comprehensive framework for resilience. These combined resources can be a source of hope, healing, and spiritual growth in challenging times.

Here's how these elements can be integrated:

Personal Loss - Growing through the Pain

- **Scripture:** Matthew 5:4 - "Blessed are those who mourn, for they will be comforted."

Personal loss is an inevitable part of the human experience: encompassing the profound grief that accompanies the death of a loved one, the end of a significant relationship, or even the loss of a cherished pet. Navigating personal loss is a multifaceted journey that requires both spiritual resilience and practical coping strategies. By intertwining faith with practical actions, we empower ourselves to navigate the storms of grief with grace and resilience.

The journey through loss is deeply personal and unique to each individual, yet by embracing the comfort of faith, seeking support from loved ones, and engaging in healing practices, we can find solace amidst sorrow and emerge stronger, with a renewed sense of hope and purpose. As we continue on this journey, may we find peace in knowing that our loved ones live on in our hearts, and that healing is a testament to the enduring power of love and faith.

- **Prayer and Meditation** - Spending time in prayer and meditation can provide clarity, peace, and strength. Lean on God's promise of eternal life and seek spiritual comfort

- **Journaling** - Writing down your thoughts and feelings to understand them more clearly can help you gain control of your emotions and improve your mental health.

- **Accept your emotions** - Allow yourself to grieve and process emotions in a healthy manner. Don't stop yourself from having a good cry if you feel one coming on.

- **Talk about it** when you can with trusted church staffers, caring friends and family members. Find solace in memories and cherish the legacy of your loved one.

- **Consider professional support,** if warranted, for grief counseling or dealing with emotions after a difficult break up.

<u>Abuse</u> - Healing from Deep Wounds

- Scripture: Psalm 34:17-18 - "The righteous cry out, and the Lord hears them; he delivers them from all their troubles. The Lord is close to the brokenhearted and saves those who are crushed in spirit."

Abuse, whether mental, physical, or sexual, is one of the most harrowing storms one can endure. Healing from abuse requires a supportive environment where survivors can express their feelings and process their trauma. Professional counseling, support groups, and a strong faith community can play vital roles in this journey.

Establish Boundaries and Safety Plans - Create clear boundaries to protect yourself from further harm. This might involve cutting off contact with the abuser, seeking legal protection, or moving to a safe environment. Developing a safety plan can provide a sense of security and control over your situation.

Practice Self-Care and Mindfulness - Practice self-care and affirm your worth through prayer and reflection. Prioritize self-care activities that promote physical, emotional, and mental well-being. This can include regular exercise, balanced nutrition, sufficient sleep, relaxation techniques, creative expression and engaging in activities that bring you joy and fulfillment.

Embrace Forgiveness As A Pathway to Healing and Liberation - Forgiveness, particularly forgiving those who have caused us harm, is perhaps one of the hardest challenges. It may seem insurmountable to forgive an abuser or someone who has deeply wronged us. Yet, forgiveness is a necessary part of healing.

It releases us from the chains of anger, resentment, and bitterness, opening the door to peace and restoration.

- **Mental abuse** often involves manipulation, gaslighting, and psychological control. It can erode a person's self-worth and create deep emotional scars, leading to anxiety, depression, and a fractured sense of self. Healing involves recognizing the abuse, seeking professional help, and rebuilding one's self-esteem through faith and support.

- **Physical abuse** leaves both visible and invisible scars, instilling fear and helplessness. The trauma from such experiences can have long-lasting effects, making it difficult for survivors to trust others and feel safe. Healing requires a safe environment, professional help, and the support of a loving community.

- **Sexual Abuse** - Molestation and rape are profoundly violating experiences that shatter one's sense of safety and personal integrity. The emotional and psychological impact is immense, often leading to feelings of shame, guilt, and unworthiness. Healing involves professional counseling, supportive relationships, and a deep connection to God's unconditional love and acceptance.

Addiction - Breaking the Chains

- **Scripture:** 1 Corinthians 10:13 - "No temptation has overtaken you except what is common to mankind. And God is faithful; he will not let you be tempted beyond what you can bear."

Addiction is a storm that can consume every aspect of a person's life. It often begins gradually but can quickly spiral out of control, affecting one's health, relationships, and overall well-being. Embrace humility and admit the need for help and support. Engage in regular prayer, scripture reading, and accountability. Seek professional treatment and support groups for addiction recovery.

- **Substance Addictions** - Alcohol and drugs are common substances that people turn to for escape, only to find themselves trapped in a cycle of dependence. Overcoming substance addiction often requires a combination of medical treatment, therapy, and support from loved ones. Faith can provide a strong foundation, offering hope and strength to break free from addiction.

- **Behavioral Addictions** - Activities such as gambling, sex, pornography, shopping, and eating can become addictive, providing temporary relief or excitement but ultimately leading to greater problems. Recognizing these behaviors as addictions and seeking professional help is crucial for recovery. Relying on God's strength and the support of a faith community can lead to lasting change for addiction recovery.

Health Issues - Battling Physical/Emotional Pain and Mental Health/Depression

- **Scripture:** Isaiah 41:10 - "So do not fear, for I am with you; do not be dismayed, for I am your God. I will strengthen you and help you; I will uphold you with my righteous right hand."

- **Scripture:** Psalms 42:11 - "Why, my soul, are you downcast? Why so disturbed within me? Put your hope in God, for I will yet praise him, my Savior and my God."

Chronic illness, injury, and other health issues are storms that test our endurance and faith. These challenges often bring physical pain, emotional distress, and a sense of helplessness. Coping involves seeking appropriate medical care and maintaining a positive outlook through faith and prayer. Scriptures like Psalms 46:1, "God is our refuge and strength, an ever-present help in trouble" can offer solace and hope during difficult times.

- **Regular Physical Activity** - Engaging in regular exercise, such as walking, jogging, yoga, or strength training can reduce stress hormones.

- **Mindfulness and Relaxation Technique**s - Practices like meditation, deep breathing exercises, progressive muscle relaxation, and mindfulness can help reduce stress.

- **Spiritual Discipline** - Embrace the present moment and trust in God's healing power. Lean on your faith community for prayer and emotional support. Strengthen your faith through regular prayer, meditation, and devotion.

- **Healthy Lifestyle Choices** - Maintaining a balanced diet, staying hydrated, getting enough sleep, and avoiding excessive consumption of alcohol, and caffeine can help manage stress levels.

- **Social Support and Communication** - Connecting with friends, family, and support groups can provide emotional support and reduce feelings of isolation. Talking about your stressors and concerns with trusted individuals can provide perspective and help you feel understood and supported.

- **Journaling** - Writing down your thoughts and feelings to understand them more clearly can help you gain control of your emotions and improve your mental health.

- **Owning A Pet** - Owning a pet can be a beneficial coping mechanism for mental health and depression issues for many people. They provide companionship, help to establish a daily routine and help with establishing a sense of responsibility with daily care. This can involve physical activity, social interaction with other pet owners, and can offer unconditional love and acceptance.

- **Seek Professional Help** - Engage with healthcare professionals, such as doctors, therapists, or specialists, who can provide medical treatment, medication and counseling.

<u>Work-Related Stresse</u>s - Finding Balance

- **Scripture:** Matthew 11:28 - "Come to me, all you who are weary and burdened, and I will give you rest."

The demands of the modern workplace can create significant stress, leading to burnout and affecting our mental and physical health. Navigating this storm involves finding a balance between work and personal life, setting boundaries, and prioritizing self-care. Faith can guide us in managing work-related stresses by reminding us of our true purpose and the importance of rest.

- **Taking time for prayer**, reflection, and spiritual growth can help us maintain perspective and avoid becoming overwhelmed. Always find comfort in prioritizing your life as God, family and work. Maintaining balance is important.
- **Foster positive relationships** with colleagues and supervisors.
- **Effective communication** and teamwork can reduce misunderstandings and conflicts.

<u>Family Conflict</u> - Healing Relationships

- **Scripture:** Ephesians 4:31-32 - "Get rid of all bitterness, rage and anger, brawling and slander, along with every form of malice. Be kind and compassionate to one another, forgiving each other, just as in Christ God forgave you."

Family conflicts are storms that can deeply affect our emotional well-being. Whether it's a strained marriage, divorce, parent-child disputes, or sibling rivalry, these issues can create a turbulent home environment. Healing family relationships requires patience, communication, and forgiveness. From a biblical perspective, Ephesians 4:32 "Be kind and compassionate to one another, forgiving each other, just as in Christ God forgave you"- encourages us to approach conflicts with grace and a willingness to forgive.

- **Open Communication** - Encourage honest and open dialogue within the family to address concerns and emotions constructively. Active listening and empathetic responses can foster understanding and mutual support.

Life Transitions - Embracing Change

- **Scripture:** Jeremiah 29:11 - "For I know the plans I have for you, declares the Lord, plans to prosper you and not to harm you, plans to give you hope and a future."

Major life transitions such as moving, changing jobs, starting at a new school or adjusting to new phases of your life can be tumultuous.

These storms challenge us to adapt to new circumstances and find stability amidst change. Embracing life transitions with faith can provide a sense of peace and direction.

Trusting that God has a plan for our lives, even when it is not immediately clear, can help us navigate these changes with confidence and hope.

- **Acceptance** - Acknowledge and accept the changes as a natural part of life. Embrace the transition rather than resisting it, allowing yourself to adapt and grow through the process.
- **Taking care of yourself** mentally, physically, and emotionally can help you navigate transitions with greater ease.
- **Seek Support and Connection** - Lean on friends, family, or support groups for guidance, encouragement, and practical assistance during transitions. Sharing your feelings and experiences with others can provide validation and perspective.

Financial Stress - Trusting in God's Provision

- **Scripture:** Philippians 4:19 - "And my God will meet all your needs according to the riches of his glory in Christ Jesus."

Financial difficulties are storms that can cause immense anxiety and fear. The pressure of debt, unemployment, or insufficient income can strain relationships and impact mental health. From a biblical standpoint, trusting in God's provision is key to overcoming financial stress.

Philippians 4:19 "And my God will meet all your needs according to the riches of his glory in Christ Jesus" reassures us that God will provide for our needs, even in times of scarcity.

- Practice wise financial stewardship and budgeting.

- Trust in God's provision and seek His guidance in financial decisions.

- Seek practical advice from financial experts and community resources.

- **Talk to someone**, talk to family members, friends, pastor, priest, or mental health professional to start venting the pressure. Getting things off your chest is often the easiest way to reduce stress and start feeling better.

- **Treat signs of addiction** - People often fall into or fall back into bad habits when extremely stressed. If you've started drinking, smoking or self-medicating because of your financial stress, get help. Look for support groups.

Integrating spiritual practices with practical coping strategies creates a holistic approach to facing life's storms. Prayer and meditation can provide inner strength and guidance, while seeking community and support offers practical assistance and encouragement.

Finding meaning in challenges and practicing gratitude fosters resilience, complemented by professional support and self-care strategies that promote emotional well-being. By maintaining a hopeful outlook and embracing both spiritual wisdom and practical tools, individuals can navigate storms with resilience and emerge stronger.

This integrated approach acknowledges the complexity of personal struggles while emphasizing the importance of faith, community, self-care, and proactive coping strategies in fostering growth and healing.

> While the storms of life are inevitable, they also offer opportunities for growth, resilience, and deeper faith. By embracing acceptance and forgiveness, seeking support, and relying on God's strength, we can navigate these challenges and emerge stronger. The journey through the storm may be grueling, but with faith as our guiding light, we can find the path to healing and peace.

By employing these and other strategies, you can navigate personal storms more effectively and emerge stronger and more prepared for future challenges. Always be relentless in your resolve to prevail during a personal storm. The storms of life should only make you stronger. Always have an "I might bend but I won't break" attitude.

Always remember that it's always darkest right before the dawning of a new day. Right before you make it through your storm of life, it may get tough but never give up, never give out and never give in. You can make it. Believe in you.

Become your biggest cheerleader. With God on your side all things are possible if you just believe. Keep moving forward, keep your head up and remember you serve a mighty God.

Chapter Three - Key Takeaways:

1) Acceptance and Forgiveness are key for the healing process.

2) Stay positive and optimistic but seek the support of friends and family.

3) Know that it's okay to seek professional support.

4) Never think that you are alone in your fight.

5) Always stay prayerful and take time to take care of yourself.

Motivational Songs:

1) "Jireh - Elevation Worship" - Maverick City / Chandler Moore

2) "You Don't Know" - Zacardi Cortez

3) "Our God" - Chris Tomlin

4) "Never Would Have Made It" - Marvin Sapp

5) "I Sing Praises" - Josue Avila / Calvary Orlando

Scripture References:

1) Psalms 32:8

2) Proverbs 3:5-7

3) Psalms 23:4-6

4) Psalms 91:1-16

Motivational Quote -

"Oftentimes God demonstrates his faithfulness in adversity by providing us what we need to survive. He does not change our painful circumstances. He sustains us through them."- **Charles Stanley**

A Prayer for "Conquering The Storm"

"Dear Heavenly Father"

In the midst of life's storms, I come before You Lord, seeking Your strength and guidance. Lord, You are the Master of the wind and the waves, and I trust in Your power to calm the storms that rage around me. Grant me courage and strength to face each challenge with faith and hope.

When fear and uncertainty threaten to overwhelm me, remind me of Your promise to never leave nor forsake me. Help me to anchor my soul in Your steadfast love and unchanging faithfulness. May Your peace, which surpasses all understanding, guard my heart and mind.

Father, I surrender my worries and anxieties into Your capable hands. Grant me wisdom to discern Your will amidst the chaos, and strength to persevere with grace. Strengthen my faith, Lord, that I may rise above the trials and testify to Your goodness and provision in every storm.

Thank You, Father, for being my refuge and strength, a present help in times of trouble. May Your glory shine through me as I trust in You to conquer every storm of life.

In the precious name of Jesus - Amen

CHAPTER NOTES

LET GO AND LET GOD

Learning How to Let go and Trust God

To me it was always difficult to release control over the issues in my life that caused me stress, anxiety, or despair, and trusting God through faith and belief in His guidance. I would always find a way to second guess God.

Recognizing that there were things in my life beyond my control was hard for me to comprehend. Relinquishing my grip or control of each situation was very difficult. It was hard trusting God. I had to begin to focus on God's word. I began to focus on Mathew 5:9-13

"Our Father which art in heaven, Hallowed would be thine name. Thy kingdom come. Thy will be done on earth as it is in heaven, Give us this day our daily bread. And forgive us our debts, as we forgive our debtors. And lead us not into temptations, but deliver us from evil: For thine is the kingdom, and the power, and the glory, forever. Amen"

I had to remind myself that God always wants what's best for us and that He has the power to change any situation in our lives.

I had to change my mindset.

I had to surrender control and start trusting God. I needed to have 'mountain moving, walk on water' faith in God.

I began to reflect on the fact that God had a plan for my life and that His timing for events in my life was perfect, even if it didn't always align with my personal timeline or my immediate desires in life.

I had to realize that I couldn't control and manage every single aspect of my life. Letting go of the outcome and trusting God, allowed me to reduce my anxiety and stress. I began focusing on the present, instead of worrying about what the future held, or trying to manipulate the outcome. I had to focus on what I could do now and leave the outcomes to God. God says to pray and don't worry.

I knew that I had to get over my fears. I had to choose faith over fear by believing in God's protection over my life and over life's situations. This led to me having a greater inner peace in so many challenging circumstances in my life.

This helped me to strengthen my faith in God, to rely on him even more and to trust that he would always be there for me and deliver me through the darkest times in my life. It helped me to understand that whatever happened was part of a greater plan for my life.

I remember having to make so many difficult decisions in my personal life and in my career of over 30 years of management. One of the most difficult decisions came in the form of a life altering decision in my personal life.

In late August of 2019 my dad was diagnosed with stage 4 lung cancer. He fought valiantly for over 6 months with numerous doctor visits and hospital stays. On March 10, 2020 he was rushed to the hospital for the final time and placed on life support. On March 11,

2020 after meeting with his doctors in the ICU it became apparent that my dad was dying. Later that day during another doctor's visit while my mom and two of my siblings were in the room the doctor mentioned the severity of his condition again. My mom broke down crying, the doctor fell to his knees and began to comfort my mom.

We later begin the difficult discussion of removing my dad from life support. I had a long discussion with my mother and with each one of my siblings. After careful consideration and consulting with the hospital staff we made the heart wrenching decision to remove my dad from life support on the following day. We each knew that my dad had fought all that he could fight, and the outcome had already been determined. To prolong his suffering and the suffering of my mom wasn't God's will. We had to let go and let God.

On March 12, 2020, my dad passed away, while holding his soulmate's hand (my mom) and was surrounded by his children. I rested my head on my dad's head as he drew his last breath. We knew that my dad had lived a Godly life and would join God in heaven with his parents and my little brother.

The timing was significant because 2 weeks later, the entire world shut down due to COVID 19.

We often tend to hold on to something that we shouldn't. We tend to try and fix something that we can't fix. God may have already given you a solution to your problem or maybe God is waiting for you to just step back and let him take care of it.

We sometimes spend a lot of time trying to change a predetermined outcome. That's why it is so important to understand God's will for your life. We are often hell-bent on opening a door that is not meant to be opened or trying desperately to close a door that is not meant to be closed.

Three words that stand out to me in the Serenity Prayer are serenity, courage and wisdom.

Serenity is a state of mental calmness and clarity. It's where you feel at peace in the present moment, and you can focus on what matters. It often refers to being in a state of tranquility, or peace. God wants you to remain serene during turbulence.

There will be times when you cannot change, alter or modify an outcome in your life. You must accept that you are powerless over the situation and only God can change the situation if and only if it's meant to change.

Having the courage to change the things that God has revealed that you can change, is being obedient to God. Having faith will give you courage. Courage means doing the right thing, being selfless and making difficult decisions.

Summon your inner strength and determination to face challenges even in the midst of fear or uncertainty. You are confident in knowing that God has prepared you for that phase or that decision in your life, the manifestation is clear and decisive.

Having wisdom is more than just being knowledgeable or intelligent. It involves having a deeper and unselfish understanding of life and people and having the ability to apply that understanding in ways that lead to better decision making and a more fulfilling life.

"One of the hardest lessons in life is letting go. Whether it's guilt, anger, love, loss or betrayal, change is not easy. We fight to hold on and we fight to let go."

Ecclesiastes 3:1-8 (NIV): "There is a time for everything, and a season for every purpose under the heavens."

Acceptance: The prayer begins with a plea for serenity to accept the things that cannot be changed. This teaches us the importance of recognizing and coming to terms with circumstances and realities that are beyond our control. It emphasizes the futility of resisting or struggling against situations that are inevitable or beyond our power to influence.

Acceptance does not imply resignation but rather a conscious decision to acknowledge reality and find peace within it.

Serenity Prayer

"God

grant me

the Serenity

to accept the things

I cannot change

the Courage

To change the things

I can, and

the Wisdom

to know the

Difference."

Letting go and letting God handle difficult issues in your life requires trust and unwavering faith. Here are 10 ways to help develop that mindset:

1) **Prayer and Meditation** - Take time out of your busy schedule to pray and meditate, surrendering your worries and concerns to the Lord. This can help you to feel more of a connection to God.

2) **Release Control** - Acknowledge that you can't control everything in your life. Acknowledge to God that you need and desire his help. Trust that God has a well laid out plan for your life even during uncertainty.

3) **Trust in God's Divine Timing** - Have faith that things will happen in the right timing. Even if things don't happen according to your schedule, trust and believe that God has a greater plan at work in your life.

4) **Surrendering Your Burdens** - Turn your worries and burdens over to the Lord. Trust that he will provide you with strength and guidance to handle anything that comes your way.

5) **Seek Guidance through Scripture** - Review scriptures for guidance, comfort and inspiration. Reflect on scriptures that speak to your current situation and help strengthen your resilience in your faith.

6) **Practice Patience** - Develop patience as you wait on God's resolution or answer to your situation. Trust that God is working behind the scenes on your behalf and that his timing will be perfect.

7) **Be Open and Trust God's Decision** - Be prepared to release any attachments to a specific outcome, even if it's different from what you had in mind. Instead focus on aligning your will to God's will and direction in any situation. Trust that God knows what is best for you. If God knows the correct number of hairs on your head, I think he definitely knows the best outcome for your situation.

8) **Stay Open and Attentive** - Listen for the Holy Spirit's guidance and direction that comes to you through prayer, meditation and even through other people.

9) **Lean on Your Faith Team** - Surround yourself with supportive people who provide prayer and support during difficult times. Value the strength and comfort of others who share your beliefs.

10) **Always Practice Gratitude** - Maintain an attitude of gratitude especially in the midst of challenges. Focus on the blessings that you already have in your life and trust that God will continue to provide for your needs.

Chapter Four - Key Takeaways:

1) It's difficult to give control of your situation to God but you must trust Him.

2) Knowing and understanding Serenity, Courage and Wisdom.

3) Focus on the present and let God focus on the outcome.

Motivational Songs:

1) "Oceans AKA Spirit Lead ME" - Hillsong United

2) "When I Pray" - Doe

3) "Living Hope" – Abigail Ginsterblum

4) "Great Are You Lord - All Sons & Daughters

5) "Let Go and Let God - Dewayne Woods

Scripture References:

1) Deuteronomy 31:6

2) Revelation 21:4-5

3) Ephesians 3:1-20

4) Proverbs 3:5

Motivational Quote -

Faith - "It does not make things easy, It makes things possible." - Luke 1:37 (paraphrased)

A Prayer for "Letting Go and Let God"

"Dear Heavenly Father"

I humbly come before You, surrendering my desires, worries, and struggles into Your loving hands. Help me, Lord, to release control over every aspect of my life and to trust completely in Your perfect plan. Teach me the beauty of letting go and letting You take charge in my life or my situation.

Forgive me for the times I have tried to handle things on my own, instead of relying on Your wisdom and guidance. Grant me the strength and courage to relinquish my fears and uncertainties to You, knowing that You are faithful and trustworthy.

Fill me with Your peace that surpasses all understanding, as I release my burdens into Your care. Help me to walk by faith, not by sight, and to rest in the assurance that Your ways are higher than my ways.

Thank You, Lord, for Your unfailing love and grace. May Your will be done in my life, and may I find joy and freedom in surrendering to Your divine plan for my life.

In the precious name of Jesus - Amen

CHAPTER NOTES

BECOMING THE BEST VERSION OF YOURSELF

Living with a purpose.
How to activate the person in you that
God wants you to be.

Having the courage to change things in your life that you can change starts with creating the change in you. Each one of us is uniquely built by God.

God has personally hand crafted our heart, mind, body, and soul. Each part of our body has a specific purpose in living a Godly life. How much better would you be if you were the best version of yourself?

Are you currently being the best version of yourself? What are you good at? What do you need to improve? What are you working on? What do you need to be working on? Do you know?

The focus of this chapter is "You."

In 2021 the total age-adjusted suicide rate in the United States increased to 14.0 per 100,000. The data showed that suicide rates among males (22.8 per 100,000) were 4 times higher than in females (5.7 per 100,000). From 2000 to 2020, more than 800,000 people died by suicide in the United States alone with over 78% being male. - Centers for Disease Control and Prevention (CDC)

A record 49,500 people died by suicide in 2022 the highest level since 1941, in the United States. The data is alarming. Just one death alone is one to many. Worldwide more than 700,000 people die by suicide every year. - (World Health Organization)

Ironically suicide attempts and suicides rates are higher in the Spring time than any other season. Just recently (May 25th of 2024) 30 year old, two-time PGA golfer Grayson Murray died by suicide.

God says in Jeremiah 29:11 – "For I know the plans I have for you, declares the Lord, plans to prosper you and not to harm you, plans to give you hope and a FUTURE."

A few years ago, my wife purchased a picture for my son and one for my daughter. It has a wonderful message. It says:

"I believe in Miracles,

I believe in the opportunity for happiness that each new day brings,

I believe in the strength provided by Family and Friendship,

I believe in the Power of Prayer,

I believe in Hope, I believe in Joy,

I believe in Love,

I believe in Me,

I believe in You."

I can only sympathize with the pain and hurt that so many people have in the world. I want to help by helping each one of us to become the best version of ourselves. I don't want us to get so caught up in determining our purpose in life that we lose sight of the daily importance of self-love.

Self-love means having a high regard for your own well-being and happiness. It also means taking care of your own needs and not sacrificing your well-being to please others. Self-love means not settling for less than you deserve.

It is absolutely important to be selfless and pour into others, but not at a cost to your own well-being. You must pour into yourself just as fervently and passionately as you pour into the lives of others around you. Your life is important, and your life absolutely matters.

Inspiring Quotes

"You are enough, just as you are."- Megan Markle

"Self-love is the key to a joyful life."- Buddha

"Be your own kind of beautiful."- Author Unknown

"You are your own priority."- Author Unknown

Self-love is the best love."- Author Unknown

'Fall in love with taking care of yourself."- Brianna Wiest

'Your love for yourself sets the standard for others."- Author Unknown

"Love yourself first and everything else falls in line." - Lucille Ball

In 2011, I was coaching my son's football team, the Titans. My wife was also the cheerleading coach. I had an experience that would forever change my life and the lives of thousands of people around me.

On one fall afternoon in late September, I found myself wrangling over what to teach during football practice. Normally I would have a practice plan drawn up to maintain the best use of our practice time. For some unknown reason, I was struggling to create a plan. We started the season winning only one game and we had managed to lose four straight games. I was at an impasse. About an hour before practice, I began to get calls from my assistant coaches, one after another.

All three had major issues going on either at work, home, or with their vehicle. At this point, I'm thinking *Lord this is not for me, I don't have the patience nor the ability to do this.*

About 15 minutes before practice was due to start, the Holy Spirit spoke to me and gave me 4 words that started with the letter "C". They were Confidence, Christ-like attitude, Character, and Commitment. God had placed on my heart to have a team meeting before practice and to discuss the four words and the meanings of each.

So, being obedient to God, that's what I set out to do. I didn't exactly know how a group of 11 and 12 year old kids would react to me talking about God and other words that they probably didn't completely understand. I called the team together before beginning warmup drills. I began to explain what was on my heart, to my amazement, the kids were very attentive the entire time. Each of them was hanging on my every word. Not one time did I mention our losing record, nor did I talk about any improvements about the team.

After explaining the meaning of each of the C-words, I asked the kids to prioritize the words which were most important to them. This was their conclusion:

The 4-C's

Christ-Like Attitude – <u>Courage</u> to always do the right thing even when it is hard and unpopular. Always display kindness, honesty, and integrity.

Commitment – Embody dedication, discipline, and sacrifice; never give up, and always be prepared.

Confidence – Believe in yourself and your abilities, Trust God and be bold.

Character – Demonstrate moral strength, strong work ethics and a reputation of excellence.

I explained to each player that going forward I wanted each of them to take these words to heart and to be the best version of themselves that God wanted them to be. I explained that each one of them had control of their own destiny, dreams, and desires.

I explained to them that we as coaches cared about each one of them and that we loved each one as though they were our own. I talked about the bond that I wanted them to have with one another on and off the field and the importance of having each other's back.

I talked about how we wanted each player to one day become responsible loving dads that their children could look up to. We discussed the importance of going to church, focusing on school and being obedient to their parents. We talked about taking responsibility for their actions and being great siblings at home. We talked about always being respectable.

I told them how proud we were of each one of them as coaches and as parents.

After meeting for about 35 minutes, we began our warm-up drills. I immediately noticed the extra excitement in the group. They were fired up and beaming with energy. I did not have assistant coaches that night, but the practice went flawlessly. It was the best practice that we had ever had.

Normally after each practice either I would say a prayer or allow one of my assistant coaches to say the closing prayer. This time I asked if anyone wanted to say a prayer. To my surprise I saw several hands raised, one of which was my own son. I asked him if he would do the honors of leading us with our closing prayer.

I vowed going forward that each one would be allowed to do a closing prayer after practice or after the game. I was so proud of each one of my players, especially my son. I could see how excited and pumped up they were.

After practice, while leaving the field with my son, I had tears of joy in my eyes. I told him how proud I was of him for stepping up with saying the prayer and stepping up in practice. I could hear the Holy Spirit whispering, "Your boys are beginning their transition to young men. Allow them to be great."

For the remainder of the season, I would often have parents walk up to me and ask what I did to make the kids act so differently. They would often say "it's like a switch came on all of a sudden, I have a different child."

We won our next 3 games, and everyone was so excited. The players, parents, and coaches were booming with enthusiasm, then *it* happened.

I received a call from the mother of one of my players. She went on to say that she was mad at her son but at the same time she was so proud of him. She explained that he was acting differently after school that day. She explained that he came up to her and started just bawling his eyes out and was filled with emotions.

After a few minutes he was able to communicate what happened. He went on to say that he did not get any sleep the night before and that he couldn't concentrate at school. He said that he just did not feel right.

After a few moments he explained that he had done something that he knew was so wrong. He had taken money from her purse without her permission and that the guilt was eating him up inside. He explained that he knew that it was wrong but did it anyway. He did not think that she would miss the money, and she did not.

His mother went on to say that she and her husband were trying to figure out the best way to manage the situation. She explained that her son had never shown emotions like that before and that he had never taken full responsibility for his actions before.

I reminded his mom about our team's conduct policy. One of the items that was clearly explained was that if a player got in trouble at home that they would be subject to punishment with the team as well. I explained to her that we wholeheartedly would support any decision that they made.

We ultimately decided to suspend the player for one game and prior to him returning for the next practice, he would have to run extra sprints.

The next day the mom brought her son to practice. Prior to the team beginning the warm-up exercises, the player apologized to the team for not being able to participate in practice nor play in the next game. He explained to the team what happened and that he had made a bad decision. The entire team surrounded him and told him that everything would be okay and that they were proud of him for having the courage to do the right thing even though it was hard.

At that moment, I realized that we as coaches, mentors and parents had done our jobs. Not because we had won three games in a row, but because we had scored a touchdown in the game of life with these young men. I was an emotional wreck for the rest of the day. I just could not stop thanking and praising God.

We went on to win the next three games that we played. It was as if we were a different team. We played in the championship game but lost by ten points to a team that was undefeated and who had previously beaten us by forty points.

Even though the loss was disappointing to the kids, they realized the value of the season. We all learned a valuable lesson that year. There was greatness inside of each one of those kids and it was up to us to find a way to help them to become the best version of themselves.

They believed in themselves, they believed in their teammates, and most importantly they believed in God.

I jokingly told my wife that this was a true "Remember the Titans" moment. The only difference is that we didn't have Denzel Washington to play my role as the head coach.

To see the emotions of the young men that they were becoming was such a blessing. So often boys or men fail to show their real emotions. We have a false perception of men not having to show vulnerability.

As parents we must teach our children, especially boys, that it's okay to show true emotions and that it is okay to ask for help. It is okay to not have all the answers, but to put their trust in God and believe that he will deliver them and that all things are possible through Jesus Christ.

As parents we have to create a culture that allows our children to not be afraid to reach out to us for help in difficult times in their lives. We have to create a culture in our homes that will allow children to understand that if they make a mistake that it's not the end of the world.

We are all broken, or have been broken, at some point in our lives. We are all looking for solutions. They don't need to be the perfect model citizen. The same grace and mercy that we extend to others on a daily basis, we need to extend to our own family.

Just to be clear, we all want the best for our children. We must understand that as much as we are working and hoping for our children's success, it is as important, sometimes more important, that we are there loving them and encouraging them through their failures and disappointments.

Without having experienced failure, it makes it so difficult to truly understand and appreciate your successes in life.

After that football season, my wife and I used the 4-Cs as our team's motivational message. We coached football, baseball, and softball for the next 7 years. We found that message to resonate with all our players and parents. I went on to use the 4-C's during high school and middle school mentoring sessions. I eventually incorporated using the 4-Cs into my management teaching style at work.

"You can be happy and still want to improve. You can be happy and still want to be healthier, smarter, more generous, and more compassionate. Because happiness isn't about complacency……it's about knowing that you are enough."- **Gretchen Rubin**

Becoming the best version of yourself involves a continuous process of self improvement, personal growth, and self discovery aimed at maximizing your potential of living a purposeful life. Here are some tips on becoming the best version of yourself. These can help you to activate the person in you that God wants you to be:

1) **Self-Awareness** - Understanding your strengths, weaknesses, values, and passions is important. It's about gaining insight into who you are and what you truly want out of life. I often used a tool called a SWOT analysis in my management career. This tool can be used as a self improvement tool. Self- SWOT analysis allows an individual to access their strengths, weaknesses, opportunities for improvements and threats.

2) **Spiritual Growth and Development** - Strengthen your daily walk with Jesus Christ in your life. Strive to live a Godly life by allowing time for daily devotion and meditation. Just take time to open up to God and ask for daily guidance and understanding. Ask God for alignment and purpose in your life.

3) **Take Care of Your Health** - Prioritize your physical, mental and emotional well-being. This should include regular exercise, healthy eating, adequate sleep, stress management, and seeking support when needed. Adopt healthy habits.

4) **Set Clear Goals** - Establishing specific, achievable goals gives you direction and motivation. These goals should be aligned with your values and aspirations, guiding you towards the life you want to create. These goals provide specific direction and purpose.

5) **Practice Resilience** - Cultivate resilience to bounce back from setbacks and adversity in life. It's about learning from all experiences and continuing to move forward with a positive

mindset. It's about looking at challenges as opportunities for growth and development, then developing coping strategies to navigate difficult times.

6) **Practice Ethical Living** - Make good choices that reflect your values and ethics. Contribute positively to your community and engage in acts of kindness and generosity to others. Find ways to make a positive impact on others through volunteering, mentoring, or advocacy. Contributing to others' wellbeing helps develop a genuine sense of connection and purpose.

7) **Live Authentically** - Be true to yourself and live in alignment with your beliefs and aspirations. This will help in pursuing goals that are meaningful to you. Live in the moment and appreciate the present for the value that it teaches.

8) **Practice Gratitude** - Develop a mindset of gratitude and appreciation for the blessings in your life. Gratitude can improve your overall well-being, increase resilience and enhance your relationships. Thank God for what you have and trust Him for what you will need.

9) **Personal Development** - Actively seek ways to develop skills, acquire knowledge and challenge yourself. Seek out new experiences that expand your knowledge and perspective. This could involve formal education, reading, learning new hobbies, enhancing career skills, or improving emotional intelligence.

10) **Improving Emotional Intelligenc**e - Emotional intelligence involves understanding and managing your own emotions, as well as empathizing with others. This skill is essential for effective communication, conflict resolution and building healthy relationships.

11) **Relationships** - Building and maintaining healthy and supportive relationships is imperative to become the best version of yourself. Surround yourself with people who lift you up and contribute positively to your growth and well-being. You also want these people to be honest and transparent as well. Surround yourself with people who will not let you fall and who want to see you succeed. Genuine people who will be there for you in your worst moments. Surround yourself with strong people who love and support you.

"The most powerful relationship you will ever have is the relationship with yourself." **- Steve Maraboli**

12) **Always find ways to laugh and have fun** - Laughter is good for the heart, mind and soul. Each time that you laugh, you breathe more deeply. This sends more oxygen into your lungs and this helps your heart pump oxygen rich blood throughout your body. A good hearty laugh relieves physical tension and stress, leaving your muscles relaxed for up to 45 minutes. **- Mayo Clinic**

Proverbs 17:22 - "A merry heart doeth good like a medicine: but a broken spirit drieth the bones."

13) **Forgiveness** - Oftentimes we lack the ability to move on from past mistakes and indiscretions. We lack the ability to forgive others and to sometimes forgive ourselves. We all have sinned and fallen short of the glory of God. He has forgiven you and allowed you to forgive yourself. Acknowledge the past but embrace the future.

Finally, always remember that personal growth and becoming the best version of yourself is a lifelong journey and will not happen overnight.

It is essential to maintain patience and perseverance. Always take a brief moment to celebrate your wins or victories along the way.

Enjoy the little things in life, for one day you will look back and realize they were the big things that really mattered.

Chapter Five - Key Takeaways:

1) Always remember that your life is important and that your life absolutely matters. Always prioritize self-love and self-care.

2) Incorporate the **4-Cs** into your daily life.

   Christ-Like Attitude – <u>Courage</u> to always do the right thing even when it is hard and unpopular. Always display kindness, honesty, and integrity.

   Commitment – Embody dedication, discipline, and sacrifice; never give up, and be prepared.

   Confidence – Believe in yourself and your abilities; trust God and be bold.

   Character – Demonstrate moral strength, strong work ethics, and build a reputation of excellence.

3) Remember that personal development and becoming the best version of yourself is a journey that will take time, patience, and perseverance. "Take time to celebrate your wins along the way to your greatness."

Motivational Songs:

1) "Because of Who You Are" - Vickie Yohe
2) "Praise The Lord" - Micah Tyler
3) "To The Table" - Zack Williams
4) "Way Maker" - Sinach

Scripture References:

1) Proverbs 21:1-5
2) Mark 12:31
3) Colossians 3:9-10
4) 2 Corinthians 5:17

Motivational Quotes -

– "Happiness is an inside job. Don't assign anyone else that much power over your life." - **Mandy Hale**

– "The most important thing is to enjoy your life- to be happy – it's all that matters." - **Audrey Hepburn**

A Prayer on "Becoming the Best Version of Yourself"

"Dear Heavenly Father"

I come before You with a heart eager to grow and to become the person You have created me to be. Thank You for loving me unconditionally and for Your desire to see me flourish in every aspect of my life.

Lord, guide me on this journey of self-improvement and transformation. Grant me wisdom to recognize areas where I need to change and the courage to take steps towards personal growth. Help me to embrace Your truth and to align my thoughts, words, and actions with Your will.

Father, empower me to let go of negative habits, attitudes, and fears that hold me back from reaching my full potential. Fill me with Your Holy Spirit, that I may bear the fruits of love, joy, peace, patience, kindness, goodness, faithfulness, gentleness, and self-control.

Help me to see myself through Your eyes, as a beloved child created in Your image. Strengthen me to persevere through challenges and setbacks, trusting that Your grace is always sufficient.

May I glorify You in all that I do, becoming a beacon of Your light and love to those around me. Thank You for Your promises and for the assurance that You will complete the good work You have started in me.

In the precious name of Jesus - Amen

CHAPTER NOTES

_____

_____

_____

_____

_____

_____

_____

_____

_____

_____

_____

_____

_____

_____

_____

_____

_____

_____

_____

_____

_____

_____

_____

_____

_____

_____

IT TAKES DISCIPLINE TO TRUST GOD

Trust God's Timing
Focus on Patience and Obedience
and Never Give Up

Having the ability to maintain faith, especially during challenging times, requires consistent effort and self-control. Trusting God requires patience and obedience. It also requires belief in His plan, and timing, for your life, even at times when immediate circumstances seem hopeless, and you can't see His presence in your life.

God remains faithful to us regardless of how many times we have fallen short of obeying his commandments. God doesn't give up on us, so why do we sometimes give up on him? The answer is clear, sometimes we lack the discipline to trust God's timing and direction in our lives.

Discipline in this instance refers to the mental and spiritual efforts required to focus on your faith and trust in God rather than giving in to doubt, fear, or impatience.

Trusting God is not always an automatic or easy action. It's a method that needs to be developed and maintained through deliberate and consistent effort. This can involve regular practices such as prayer, meditation, reading scriptures, or other forms of daily worship. Trust God to give you what you need and to finish the work that He began in you. Oftentimes obedience is a minute-by-minute process to put one foot in front of the other. We need to make the task smaller and be faithful in each small step of the way. Always trust God's unfailing and unwavering love for what comes next. This also means actively choosing to rely on your faith as a guiding principle for making decisions and handling life's ups and downs, rather than solely relying on your own understanding or external advice.

It takes self-discipline to deny your human nature of giving up or giving in to something other than living the way God wants you to live with faith and hope. It's a lifelong practice, regardless of where you are in your faith journey.

In the Bible, Jesus tested Peter's faith and obedience by granting Peter's request and allowing him to walk on the water. As long as Peter's faith and obedience was true and pure, he was able to walk on the water, but when Peter saw and felt the boisterous wind he became afraid and began to sink. He immediately cried out to Jesus saying, "Lord save me." Immediately Jesus stretched forth his hand and saved him and said, "O thou of little faith, wherefore didst thou doubt?" - Matthew 14:24-34.

Unfortunately, we live in a world that wants everything right now. If we can't physically see it happening right now, we don't trust that it will happen. In some cases, as soon as we face a little turbulence or resistance, we want to give up. That's where the discipline comes in.

One of my favorite quotes about discipline comes from my favorite boxer of all time, "Iron" Mike Tyson: "Discipline is doing what you hate to do but doing it like you love it." You will give up on your slightest struggle without discipline.

The lesson with Peter is simple: we must have the courage to step out on faith and obey God, knowing that He will carry you through and He will help you to overcome any fear or disbelief that Satan puts in our path. In short, keep your eyes focused on Jesus.

Many of us either are struggling with or have struggled with maintaining some form of discipline in our lives. Establishing and maintaining discipline requires courage, perseverance and resilience. My challenge to you is this: don't blame God for the lack of discipline in your life. Hold yourself accountable first and foremost.

Let's talk a little more about discipline itself.

<u>What is Discipline?</u>

Discipline is a process.

Discipline is a mindset.

Discipline is a habit.

Discipline is hard.

Discipline is a culture change.

Discipline is faith in action.

Discipline is rewarding.

Discipline is hearing and believing in God.

Having discipline takes faith.

Establishing discipline in your daily life is crucial to establishing discipline in your spiritual life. Often we struggle to have discipline in our finances, health, business, etc. and we look to place blame on everyone except ourselves.

I remember reading a quote some time ago, that stated:

"Discipline makes today harder but tomorrow easier." If you're serious about changing your life you will find a way. If not, you will find an excuse. "Excuses make today easier, but make tomorrow harder."- **Hal Elrod**

In September of 2023, I was faced with a very difficult decision in my life. I was having the best year of my professional career and would soon be up for a promotion. As I mentioned earlier, in March of 2020 my mom lost her soul mate of over 67 years: her husband, my dad. Although she was devastated, she did not give up.

Her health began to rapidly deteriorate and, as a result, she was in and out of the hospital for over three years. Her faith remained strong even in her most challenging times during her hospital stays. She would often thank God for all of her 11 children, her 30 grandchildren and her 38 great grandchildren. She trusted God for his miraculous healing power.

Despite her best efforts she still struggled with health issues and needed additional support with her daily care. I was faced with the decision of leaving my job to help my mom and trusting God with my future.

In early August of 2023, God spoke to me and told me that September would be my last month with my employer.

Have you ever tried to reason with God? Or maybe it's just me. I remember asking God the following questions: "God so what about my income, what about my mortgage, what about my son and daughter who were both in college, what about my ruptured disc in my neck?" There was absolute silence. Then I could hear the Holy Spirit ask me a simple question, "Have I ever failed you?"

I could hear God re-assuring me that he would never leave me nor forsake me. He told me that he had bigger plans for my life, and that I should continue to trust him.

So, after providing my three-week notice period, in September of 2023, I stepped out on faith and left my employer, whom I had spent the last 20 years with. Ending a lucrative 33-year career in management. I had to trust God with my life, my career and the season of my life that I was in.

I had to quickly pivot my focus. I was on a mission with my siblings to help my mom take control of her health. We began to focus on her physical and mental well-being. We consulted with all of her doctors.

- We established and implemented a balanced diet for my mom.
- We evaluated her medical care and evaluated her medication list.
- We helped establish an exercise and fitness routine with her medical care team.
- We made sure that she was provided wellness and emotional care support to help conquer her storm of losing her soulmate of 67 years.

As of June 2024, I am so proud to say that despite numerous health concerns, old and new, my mom has managed to lose over 33 lbs. and is doing significantly better with zero hospital stays for over a year.

She has remained self-disciplined in her health and wellness improvement plan and has begun to do the things that she previously enjoyed doing all of her life, like quilting, attending church services and spending quality time with her family.

"True faith manifests itself through our actions." - **Francis Chan**

The second part of this story is my personal health journey. I made the decision to also take control of my health and well-being. During the same time period, I managed to lose 16 lbs. through proper diet and exercise.

In November of 2012, I was in a serious car accident and damaged 3 discs in my neck. In December of 2014, despite having gone through physical therapy and other pain management activities, I could barely walk.

I had to undergo a three-layer cervical fusion surgery to repair the damaged discs in my neck. The surgery was successful but fast forward to August of 2022 when I ruptured another disc below the previously repaired discs in my neck. The pain was intense.

I was presented with two options by my neurosurgeon, surgery or physical therapy (PT). I chose PT.

For the next 18 months, I worked relentlessly with my PT team to strengthen the core muscles in and around my neck and back. The Bible says in Romans 4:17, "to call those things that aren't, as though they are, until they come to be," and that's exactly what I did. I knew that I needed a miraculous healing and that God would deliver me through this painful storm in my life. I began to claim my healing.

James 2:17 - "So also faith by itself, if it has no works, is dead." I realized that I had to put in the hard work and sacrifices to change my situation. In February of 2024, I gradually began to start jogging again for the first time in over 12 years.

In March of 2024, I was released from PT and my neurosurgeon, without having surgery. Let me tell you, God is truly Amazing.

On April 13, 2024 I ran in my first 5k race in over 13 years. Not just one, but two races on the same day. One at 8:00 a.m. and the second later that day at 6:00 p.m. in two different cities. I am a true testament of the goodness and mercy of God. I went from excruciating pain and discomfort to miraculously running in not just one but two races in one day with little to no pain and with competitive times of 30.20 minutes and 31.35 minutes, respectively.

My mom actually participated in the 8:00 a.m. activity as well. My mom, 2 siblings and I participated in the one-mile fun run and walk. My mom walked with her walker for about 200 yards and turned around and went back to the finish line.

She was joined by several people from the sidelines who were inspired by her determination. She was greeted by a flurry of cheers and hugs as she crossed the finish line. The local newspaper posted pictures of her heroism. She was so excited and we were all so proud of her accomplishments.

My challenge to you is: don't put off until tomorrow what you should address today. Don't procrastinate, don't delay in making a decision that impacts your life and the lives of others. Maintain the discipline necessary to change your life in a positive way.

My obedience to God has served many purposes but most importantly:

I had to trust God with boldness when deciding to take on my mom's health care improvement plan.

I had to step out on faith in my pursuit of a solution for my own health circumstances.

I had to trust God in leaving my career in management to pursue his greater calling for my life as an Author, Motivational Speaker and Business Management Consultant.

Finally, I had to understand the purpose behind God wanting me to write this book. I began to understand the need to help save souls by helping people grow closer to God and to help save lives by helping people to believe in themselves, believe in God, and believe in others.

It truly does take discipline to trust God, but look at what happens when you do!!! Lives can be changed, healing can take place, and provisions can be made.

Here are some ways to instill and maintain basic and spiritual disciplines in your life:

5 Ways to Maintain Discipline in Your Daily Life

1) **Stay Organized** - Keep your working and personal spaces clean, neat and orderly. Use planners and tracking tools effectively.

2) **Establish Clear and Effective Goals** - Outline "SMART" goals: Specific, Measurable, Actionable, Relevant, and Time Bound. Share these goals with a friend or family member to help with accountability.

3) **Establish Routines and Time Management**- Create daily schedules and habits to maintain consistency and structure in your daily activities including time spent on social media.

4) **Practice Self-Control** - Learn to resist temptations and distractions by staying aware of your priorities and staying focused and committed to your goals.

5) **Reflect and Adjust Periodically** - Regularly review your progress, recognize your achievements and identify areas needing improvements or additional concentration.

Establishing and maintaining basic discipline in your life go hand and hand in establishing and maintaining your spiritual discipline.

Here are some examples of spiritual disciplines that will allow you to become closer to God and to allow you to feel more comfortable trusting Him:

7 Ways to Build Spiritual Disciplines in Your Life

1) **Prayer** – Is a way to meet with God and unload burdens, confess, give thanks, and praise God. Praying should be a lifestyle or daily routine. Prayer is a way to make room to allow God to provide a spiritual breakthrough in your life.

2) **Worship and Obedience** – Is a way to show your love, honor and obedience to God and to acknowledge and celebrate God's power and perfection. Stay consistent when challenges come your way. Consistency helps build character. Never grow weary of doing what God is calling you to do.

3) **Devotion** – Is taking daily quiet time praying, reading God's word, and reflecting on your personal relationship with Him.

4) **Fasting** - Is a way to feed your spirit instead of your flesh and draw you nearer to God. Fasting can provide a sense of clarity and direction in your life. It can also strengthen your relationship with Christ.

5) **Solitude** – Is a time of rest and refreshment, focusing on being alone with God without distractions. The purpose is to pray, meditate on scripture, and enjoy God's presence. Jesus often took time to separate himself from his family and his disciples

and to pray early in the morning and various times throughout the day. This can be useful in strengthening your ability to resist temptations.

6) **Service** – Get involved in your church: being in the presence of other faithful believers helps build your resilience. Make time to find a community of believers who you can trust, confide in, and confess your struggles. Having people in your corner to help you with accountability and helping you to remain spiritually disciplined is essential. It is vital to pray and care for people in your community to help meet their needs.

7) **Bible Study** – Read and apply the Bible to your daily life. It is important to have first-hand knowledge of the word of God. Reading and gaining an understanding of God's word is essential in your daily walk with God.

God doesn't need to wait until you have a full understanding of his plan. When you allow yourself to fully trust him you will realize that you don't have to understand where you are going. All that matters is that he is leading and guiding you into your destiny and purpose.

What is truly meant for you will never pass you by.

Chapter Six - Key Takeaways:

1) Trusting God requires patience and obedience.

2) Discipline is hearing and believing in God. Having discipline takes faith.

3) Discipline is faith in action. Faith without works is dead. You will need to put in the work to help change your circumstances.

Motivational Songs:

1) "Trust In God" - Aware Worship (Featuring Mark Guitierrez)
2) "Wait On The Lord" - Elevation Worship & Maverick City
3) "I Will Wait" - Bri Babineaux
4) "I'll Find You" - Lecrae & Tori Kelly

Scripture References:

1) Matthew 14:24-34
2) 1 Timothy 4:7
3) Matthew 17:20
4) Hebrews 11:7

Motivational Quotes -

– "Oftentimes God demonstrates his faithfulness in adversity by providing us what we need to survive. He does not change our painful circumstances. He sustains us through them."-
  Charles Stanley

– "Faith is living and unshakable confidence, a belief in God so assured that man would die a thousand deaths for its sake."
  Martin Luther

A Prayer for "It Takes Discipline to Trust God"

Dear Heavenly Father

I come before You humbly, acknowledging Your authority over my life and trusting in Your perfect timing. Help me to surrender my desires and plans to You, knowing that Your ways are higher and Your timing is perfect. Give me the patience to wait for Your unfolding of events, even when it seems difficult or uncertain.

Lord, grant me the strength to obey Your will wholeheartedly, even when it requires stepping out in faith or enduring trials. Give me the wisdom to discern Your voice amidst the noise of the world, and the courage to follow Your path faithfully.

Father, instill in me a spirit of perseverance and determination, that I may never give up on the dreams and purposes that You have placed in my heart. When challenges arise and obstacles seem impossible to overcome, remind me of Your promises and Your faithfulness.

Thank You, Lord, for Your unfailing love and grace that sustain me through every season of life. May I walk in obedience and trust, knowing that You are with me always, guiding me towards Your best for my life.

In the precious name of Jesus - Amen

CHAPTER NOTES

TRUSTING GOD'S TIMING IN YOUR MARRIAGE

Get Ready to Receive Your Blessings

If you are like me, you can count many times you have almost given up on something only to realize that your blessing was right around the corner or 5 mins away. How often do we just sit with our fingers on the panic button, self-destruct button, or just ready to throw in the towel at the first sign of conflict?

I truly think our minds are conditioned for the worst outcomes in every situation. In some cases, we simply choose to take the easy way out. We have to remind ourselves that just because we see a few clouds forming in the sky, that doesn't always mean it's about to rain.

One of the easiest things to do in life is to quit. Today we sometimes make it easy to give up, give out, or to give in. We often give up too easily on our marriage, give out waiting on our breakthrough, or give in to outside influences and temptations that may ultimately destroy our marriage.

There are so many Bible verses in reference to marriage. Just for initial conversation, I will reference two of the following:

Genesis 2:24 - "Therefore shall a man leave his father and his mother and hold fast to his wife, and they shall become one flesh."

1 Corinthians 13:4-7 - "Love is patient and kind; love does not envy or boast; it is not arrogant or rude. It does not insist on its own way; it is not irritable or resentful; it does not rejoice at wrongdoing, but rejoices with the truth. Love bears all things, believes all things, hopes all things, endures all things."

With these scriptures in mind, where are we missing the boat in society?

According to the U.S. Census Bureau's statistics on divorce, there are over 2 million new marriages and over 900,000 new divorces each year in the U.S.

Divorce Statistics

Overview of statistics of divorce in the U.S.:

1) There are over 900,000 **divorces** in the U.S. yearly, with over 2M marriages.

2) In the U.S., there is one divorce every **30 seconds**, 108 per hour, and 2,600 per day.

3) About 42% - 45% of all first marriages in the U.S. **end in divorce**.

4) 69% of all divorces in the U.S. are **initiated** by women, 31% by men.

5) The average **duration** of marriage that ends in divorce is 13 years.

6) The average **age** for people going through a divorce is 41 years old.

7) The average **cost** of a divorce in the U.S. is $19,458 per couple.

8) Lack of commitment (73%) and constant arguing (55%) are the top **reasons** for divorce.

9) 1 in 3 divorced custodial parents doesn't receive any **child support** payments.

With this being said, let's take a bite of this elephant. Let's get started.

Trusting God in your marriage is based on having a foundation built on faith, love and mutual respect. At the center of this trust is the belief that God has brought individuals together for a biblical purpose greater than themselves. God is always willing to be involved in guiding and sustaining your union, but only at your request.

Trusting God in your marriage means acknowledging His power and wisdom in bringing two people together. This involves surrendering personal desires and ambitions to God's plan, trusting that He knows what's best for each person individually and for the marriage as a whole. This trust should create a framework where decisions, regardless of being big or small, are made with faith that God's guidance will lead to continued unity and healthy marital growth.

Trusting and honoring God in marriage empowers couples to navigate challenges and uncertainties with relentless confidence. Difficulties or rough patches in your marriage such as communication breakdown, financial pressure, or differences in expectations can strain relationships, but leaning on God's strength allows spouses to face these challenges together. Trusting in God's provision and guidance encourages couples to seek solutions with patience, humility, sincerity and a willingness to learn and grow from each experience.

Trusting God in your marriage should foster an atmosphere of grace and forgiveness while recognizing that each spouse is imperfect and will inevitably make mistakes. Trusting in God's unconditional love and forgiveness enables couples to extend the same grace to each other. This should create an environment where transparency, vulnerability, and mutual support can flourish, strengthening the marital bond. I am also a true believer in not frustrating the goodness of God. Individuals should strive to never repeat the <u>same</u> bad decisions or poor judgment that leads to disruptions in the marriage.

Trusting God in your marriage involves daily commitment and dedication to love and the Godly principles of marriage. This should shape how couples communicate, make decisions, and resolve conflicts. Ultimately, this will deepen their connection and allow their marriage to reflect the love and grace of God while also helping their marriage to be more resilient, fulfilling, and more in alignment with God's design for their lives.

Stop running from God and start running towards God. Stop taking bad advice from everybody else and take advice from God, the true source of your daily inspiration. Friends and family may not have all details of life situations at their disposal enabling them to provide bad advice.

In the case of domestic violence or abuse it is imperative that you immediately seek professional support, including but not limited to: law enforcement, family members, counseling, and medical support.

Lack of communication is a significant contributor to the lack of commitment and constant arguing identified in the data detailing the top reasons for divorce.

Good communication is a critical part of a successful marriage. Unfortunately, many couples are unable to effectively communicate their needs and desires, leading to tension and resentment. Inadequate communication can lead to miscommunication, hurt feelings, and a breakdown in trust. All of this can eventually lead to a lack of intimacy and/or infidelity.

To communicate in a marriage, couples should practice active listening and be open and honest with each other.

"Trust takes years to build seconds to break and forever to repair."
- **Dhar Mann**

When trust is violated, couples must rebuild it and foster an environment of openness and honesty.

Marriages in the Bible offer various lessons and inspiration, such as faithfulness, resilience, partnership, mutual respect, and obedience to God's will, which continue to guide and inspire couples in their journeys of marriage even today.

For example, Joseph and Mary exemplified a marriage marked by obedience to God and trust in His plan. Despite the challenges they faced, including the unconventional circumstances of Jesus' birth, they supported and cared for each other while fulfilling their roles in God's redemptive plan (Matthew 1-2, Luke 1-2).

Now how many of us men would have accepted the fact that our wife was pregnant while still being a virgin and never having had sex with you? But Joseph's faith and trust in God and trust in Mary prevailed in the end.

But there are also examples of conflicts in marriage that were self-induced and resulted in being disobedient to God which in turn caused hardship in their marriage by not waiting patiently as God's plan unfolded.

For example, Abraham and Sarah's marriage is characterized by faithfulness and resilience. Despite challenges and trials, including infertility and relocation, they remained devoted to each other and to God's plan for their family (Genesis 12-25).

Unfortunately, along the way Sarah, in essence, hit the panic button. She grew impatient and suggested to Abraham that he should have a child with her servant, Hagar, which he did, conceiving Ishmael. God reaffirmed His promise directly to her and true to his word, Sarah conceived and had a son named Isaac in their old age thereby fulfilling God's promise of a miraculous birth as promised in (Genesis 21:1-7). Hagar and Ishmael both suffered unnecessarily as a result of Sarah's impatience, initial doubt, and lack of belief.

Challenges in marriages can come in various forms. Things happen so quickly that can and will have a direct impact for the rest of your life.

My wife and I dated for 7 years prior to our marriage. I had the honor of spending time with her dad (my father-in-law) prior to our marriage. One of the happiest days of our lives was September 5, 1998, the day of our wedding. My wife had the honor of being escorted down the aisle by her dad. Fast forward 7 weeks after we were married to October 26, 1998. This would become one of the saddest days of our lives.

Around 1:30 a.m. my wife received a call indicating that her dad had suffered a massive heart attack and was in critical condition as he was rushed to the hospital. As we traveled the 25-minute drive to the hospital, I struggled to find the right words to comfort my wife. I was scared and nervous because I knew the bond that she had with her dad and how much she loved him. I couldn't bear the thought of us losing someone that meant so much to us both, especially my wife. I just couldn't imagine our lives without him.

Unfortunately, upon our arrival we learned that he had unexpectedly and tragically passed away and was no longer with us. I remember my wife as she desperately tried to hold back her emotions as she and I comforted her mom and her siblings.

This moment forever shaped our lives and created a void in our lives that I knew I could never fill. Regardless of how hard a husband tries he cannot erase the pain felt from his spouse losing her parents. Most women are deeply connected to their mom and their dad. For the next 25 years I tried desperately to comfort my wife and to help her through her grieving process. Even after having our two wonderful children in 2001 and 2004 we still struggled with communication issues.

I can remember a humbling experience that my wife and I had back in 2012. I would often call a family meeting with my family to discuss things like allowances, expectations, and upcoming vacation ideas. One day, I remember seeing notes placed throughout the house. The notes indicated that we were having a family meeting later that day.

I asked my wife about the note, and she indicated that our 8-year-old daughter wanted to have a family meeting and that she had written the notes and placed them throughout our home. One of the rules that we had established was that anyone could call a family meeting.

When it was time for the meeting, our 8-year-old daughter and 11-year-old son had prepared snacks for the meeting and a list of things to talk about. **They** had prepared a list of top priorities for our home, it included:

- Pray every day
- Believe in each other and God
- Love each other

- Stop arguing

- Have faith in others

- Encourage each other

- Be polite

- Be patient

- Tell the truth

- Have fun

- Listen to your heart

- Don't talk when others are talking

- Share

- Spend more time together

- Communicate more

- Go on a picnic or something

Wow, this was their list staring us right dead in the face. It was a humbling experience but also a wonderful moment that helped my wife and I to love and cherish our children and each other even more. We all promised to adhere to the rules.

After my dad passed in 2020, I could now sympathize more with my wife's loss of her dad. I could truly feel how it meant to lose a parent. Unfortunately, there was still a void and still some rough patches in our marriage. Then it happened!!! In the fall of 2023, my wife and I were having a friendly conversation and we touched base about visiting her dad's grave site.

I asked her if it would be ok for the kids and I to go with her to visit her dad's grave site. For the first time, she explained why she needed to go by herself. Until that moment, I truly didn't get it.

There was a part of the healing process that my wife had to deal with and was trying to deal with on her own. I thought that I was being helpful by always asking to go with her but it was really being intrusive. I finally understood my failure. The communication failure was real. There was a lack of communication from my wife in expressing her feelings: pain, hurt and the need to self-heal. But most importantly, there was a miscommunication on my part. I didn't ask the right question. I just assumed that what I was trying to do was the correct way to approach the situation. I thought that I had all of the right answers. Wow, was I wrong!

Our marriage is one of the lucky ones. We didn't let our communication issues lead to additional pain and ultimately a divorce. Although we could have saved ourselves a lot of headaches and discomfort throughout our 25 years of marriage, our unity managed to overcome the barriers that we faced. With open communication and the proper dialogue, most communication issues in a marriage can be resolved.

God constantly reminds us that the discomforts that we face don't compare to the joy that is coming our way.

God always makes us let go of something before he allows us to take hold of something better and new.

So many people are walking around holding onto pain, hurt, and frustration, so when God sends good things their way they can't catch them because they are still holding onto everything and everybody who hurt them. If they release the pain that's in their hands and heart, then God can release what's in his hands and replace the pain with joy in their heart.

Life is a never-ending journey. Everything is beautiful and special in its time. Things are anointed for a season. That season of our lives reminded me that whenever you are overwhelmed by life, you need to retreat to your prayer closet. That is always a place of refuge and solace. Always let your lonely places be turned into your holy spaces so that in times of loneliness, when you feel like you are all by yourself, you can simply invite the Holy Spirit into your darkness to rest, rule, and abide with you. Allow God to be a part of your healing process.

Philippians 4:13 reminds us that "I can do all things through Christ who strengthens me." We must always seek God's strength to overcome any obstacles that we may face. With him you can conquer anything.

Even though our marriage wasn't a divorce statistic, so many other marriages do suffer similar situations and do ultimately end in divorce. The greater calling that God has on my life is to use this and other testimonials throughout this book to help other people through life situations.

Building a successful marriage involves creating a relationship that honors God's principles and fosters spiritual growth and unity between spouses.

Here are helpful items to use in your "Marriage Toolkit" combining biblical principles with practical advice to help strengthen your marriage and your relationship:

Biblical Principles:

1) **Foundation of Faith** - Build your marriage on a foundation of faith in God and His principles (Matthew 7:24-27).

2) **Communication** - Practice open, honest, and respectful communication (Ephesians 4:29).

3) **Love and Respect** - Embody Christ-like love and mutual respect in your relationship (Ephesians 5:25-33).

4) **Forgiveness** - Extend forgiveness as freely as you have received it from God (Colossians 3:13).

5) **Unity** - Strive for unity and oneness in your marriage, aligning your goals and decisions (Ephesians 4:3).

6) **Servant Leadership** - Husbands should lead sacrificially and wives should support and respect their husbands (Ephesians 5:22-24, 1 Peter 3:1-7).

7) **Prayer** - Pray together regularly, seeking God's guidance and blessings for your marriage (Philippians 4:6).

8) **Grow Spiritually Togethe**r - Encourage each other's spiritual growth. Attend church together, participate in spiritual retreats or workshops, and discuss spiritual insights and experiences.

Practical Advice:

1) **Quality Time** - Prioritize spending quality time together regularly, away from distractions.

2) **Date Nights** - Schedule regular date nights to nurture romance and connection.

3) **Conflict Resolution** - Learn and practice healthy conflict resolution skills, such as active listening and seeking compromise. Listen twice as much as you talk. You don't have to <u>win</u> or be <u>right</u> in every conversation.

4) **Financial Planning** - Develop and stick to a budget together, aligning financial goals and priorities.

5) **Shared Responsibilities** - Divide household responsibilities equitably and support each other in daily tasks.

6) **Support Networks** - Build a supportive network of family, friends, and mentors who encourage and strengthen your marriage.

7) **Continual Learning** - Invest in marriage enrichment through workshops, retreats, or reading books on marriage.

8) **Health and Wellness** - Prioritize physical, emotional, and spiritual health for both partners.

9) **Celebrate Milestones** - Celebrate achievements and milestones in your marriage to foster gratitude and joy.

10) **Never Stop Growing** - Commit to continual growth individually and as a couple, adapting to life's changes and challenges.

11) **Always listen with an open and humble heart when feedback is being provided. Whether it's from your spouse or from your loving children.**

By integrating biblical principles with practical advice, couples can build a strong foundation that honors God and strengthens the bond with one another. This can help couples with navigating challenges and experiencing increased fulfillment and intimacy in their relationship.

"A successful marriage isn't the union of two perfect people. It's that of two imperfect people who have learned the value of forgiveness and grace." - **Darlene Schacht**

Chapter Seven - Key Takeaways:

1) **Trusting God** in your marriage is based on having a foundation built on faith, love and mutual respect.

2) **Good communication** is a critical part of a successful marriage. To properly communicate in a marriage, couples should practice active listening and be open and honest with each other. Try listening more than you talk.

3) **Prioritize your marriage** - Make time for each other amidst life's demands.

4) Prioritize regular date nights and quality time to nurture your relationship.

Motivational Songs:

1) "Forever" - Jason Nelson

2) "Gonna Be Alright" - Ryan Ellis

3) "My Life Is In Your Hands" - Kirk Franklin

4) "Dance With My Father Again" - Luther Vandross

Scripture References:

1) Genesis 2:24

2) Psalms 37: 3-5

3) Matthew 7:24-27

4) 1 Corinthians 13:4-7

Motivational Quotes-

"A happy marriage is a long conversation which always seems too short." - **Andrea Maurois**

A Prayer on "Trusting God in Your Marriage"

Dear Heavenly Father

I come before You with gratitude for the gift of marriage, a union ordained by You. Help me to trust in Your perfect timing in every season of our relationship. Grant me patience to wait for Your guidance and wisdom, especially during times of uncertainty or challenges.

Lord, strengthen our bond with Your love and grace. Help us to persevere through trials, knowing that Your plan for our marriage is good and purposeful. Give us the courage to face difficulties together, with faith in Your ability to heal and restore.

Father, deepen our commitment to each other and to You. May we always seek Your will and follow Your ways in our marriage. Grant us humility to forgive and grace to love unconditionally, reflecting Your love for us.

Thank You, Lord, for Your faithfulness and presence in our marriage. May Your peace guard our hearts and minds, and may Your joy be our strength. Guide us in building a strong foundation of trust and perseverance, rooted in You.

In the precious name of Jesus - Amen

CHAPTER NOTES

_____

_____

_____

_____

_____

_____

_____

_____

_____

_____

_____

_____

_____

_____

_____

_____

_____

_____

_____

_____

_____

_____

TRUSTING GOD'S TIMING AT WORK

Get Ready to Receive Your Blessings

For many people, one of life's biggest struggles is work life balance. If you are like me, I'm passionate about all three, God, family, and work. Throughout my career, I have always prided myself on trying to maintain prioritization in my life. For me it is God, family then work, but it hasn't always been that way. I had to sometimes learn the hard way.

Many people tend to live a double life. They are totally different at work than they are at home. You can be a success at work but a disaster at home. Some people are the total opposite. They are wonderful spouses and parents but struggle at work.

Sometimes, regardless of how hard we try, we tend to take bad work experiences home and bring challenging home concerns to work. We are all human and many of us may struggle separating the two.

In today's fast paced work environment, in the middle of meeting deadlines, attending meetings, and performing daily tasks, it can be easy to lose sight of the spiritual aspects of our lives. However, integrating faith into our professional careers not only enriches our personal spiritual journey but also enhances our workplace interactions and ultimately job performance.

It is imperative that you strive to maintain balance between your work commitments and your spiritual life. Always make time for prayer, meditation, and spiritual renewal outside of your work hours. Pray even before you make it to work, on your daily commute, in the parking lot, or wherever you feel comfortable.

I would normally do devotion early in the morning, immediately after getting up. I also read a daily devotional journal upon my arrival to work every morning. I would have my daily journal and my bible laid out on my desk every day, all day.

Sometimes it can be difficult to maintain your spiritual beliefs when you are pulled in multiple ethical and unethical ways, so you need to be prayed up and ready to go. You may be tempted to take short cuts or to compromise your values. But you have to maintain your ethical discipline.

"Do the right thing, the right way, at the right time, all the time."
- **Nick Saban**

People need to know what you stand for at work, at home, and at church. Your values should look the same regardless of your location. View your work as a means of serving others and fulfilling God's purpose. Seek opportunities to uplift and support those around you, demonstrating love through your daily actions.

Honor God through your actions and decisions. Never compromise your integrity, always be honest and fair in all your activities. Let your co-workers witness your commitment to ethical conduct and respect for others, reflecting the values taught by God. Your honesty and integrity become a testament to God's presence in your professional life.

There are several verses to reference honoring God with your spiritual work ethic. Here are two to reference:

-**Proverbs 16:3** - "Commit your work to the Lord, and your plans will be established."

-**Colossians 3:23-25** - "Whatever you do, work heartily, as for the Lord and not for men. Knowing that from the Lord you will receive the reward of the heritance, for ye serve the Lord Christ. But he that doeth wrong shall receive for the wrong which he hath done, and there is no respect of person.

Trusting God's timing at work is a journey of faith and purpose. It influences our commitment to integrity and ethical standards. Upholding honesty, fairness and compassion in our interactions and decisions reflects our trust in God's commandments and His ultimate desire for us all to live with ethical integrity in all areas of our lives.

Trusting God's timing in your work life can be seen in multiple biblical examples as well.

– **Joseph in Potiphar's House** - (Genesis 39): Joseph, sold into slavery by his brothers, found himself working in the household of Potiphar, an Egyptian official. Despite his circumstances, Joseph remained faithful and diligent in his work. He trusted God's plan and continued to honor God in his duties, eventually gaining favor and responsibility within Potiphar's household. Despite temptations to compromise his morals and personal values, he remained honorable. Even when falsely accused and imprisoned he remained dedicated.

He continued being diligent in his work and eventually was sought out for his work by Pharaoh. Even after being given power and authority by Pharaoh, he remained humble. Remarkably, he even showed grace and mercy to his brothers during the famine.

Draw strength from your faith in God, despite workplace pressure and demands. Trusting God at work means relying on his strength to overcome stress, exhaustion, and discouragement. Through prayer and reliance on His promises, find renewed energy and resilience to fulfill your responsibilities with excellence.

Your goal is to always be known as a man or woman of integrity and professionalism. Build a reputation of excellence.

Trusting God's timing involves patience and perseverance during seasons of waiting and uncertainty.

Trust that His timing is perfect and that He is working behind the scenes for your good. Patiently endure challenges and setbacks like Joseph did, knowing that they are all opportunities for God to demonstrate His faithfulness in your life.

Oftentimes people get impatient while waiting on promotion opportunities in the workplace. Always wait patiently, continuing to support people who may have received their opportunities before you.

Understand that delays and setbacks only strengthen your faith and character, preparing you for greater responsibilities and opportunities that are coming your way. Keep moving forward with excellence and professionalism. This line of thinking helped me to become a better person and ultimately made me a better employee.

Always align your career aspirations with God's purpose and blessings. Before you ask the Lord for anything, always show gratitude and thank him for everything. He knows what you need before you even ask. Things happen in order in your life for a reason.

During my 33 years of working in Corporate America, I received many awards, recognition, various accolades and promotions. Consequently, I also suffered many setbacks and delays in my professional career. I oftentimes felt overlooked for additional career advancement opportunities. I didn't grow a bitter attitude nor did I neglect my responsibilities. If anything, that made me press forward with an even greater pursuit of excellence.

"It is your reaction to adversity, not the adversity itself, that determines how your life story will develop." - **Dieter F. Uchtdorf**

I maintained an attitude of gratitude, knowing that doors were being closed for a reason and a season and that in due time, I would be elevated to a higher role in life and in my professional career. As a result of my obedience, I would often receive favor and blessings beyond belief for myself and my various work groups. I learned to put God first and to always strive to elevate people around me.

In September of 2023, my decision to leave my employer was made easier based on the fact that God had already elevated my mind to think of the big picture. In 2019, I made it my personal goal to prepare my team, my co-workers and any employee that I came in contact with for their opportunity for advancement. I felt an obligation and a passion to give back what I had learned through my many years of dedicated service and ethical workplace collaborations.

When you serve a higher purpose, your actions speak louder than your words. People look at how you react to setbacks and failures, but they also look at how you handle success and favor. Always maintain humility and grace. When you live and work for God, you uphold a higher standard of excellence. Your personal career goals are superseded by an inner desire and passion to be a servant leader.

I took great comfort coaching my team and mentoring my co-workers in our daily pursuit of creating and maintaining an ethical workplace environment. Allowing each one to value God, family and work. I felt a sense of fulfillment and accomplishment, knowing that my departure was only physical. The sense of workplace integrity that I had maintained throughout my career was reflected in my team and my co-workers. I could see work/life balance at play all around me. I was thankful to be a blessing in the lives of my team and my co-workers.

Often your blessings come in the form of you being a blessing to someone else.

Trusting God's timing at work involves developing deep faith and reliance on His guidance and provision, especially when facing uncertainties, setbacks, or waiting periods. Here are 8 practical ways to trust God's timing in your professional life:

1) **Seek God's Will** - Regularly align your career goals and aspirations with God's will through prayer and studying Scripture. Proverbs 16:3 encourages us to "Commit to the Lord whatever you do, and he will establish your plans."

2) **Pray for Guidance** - Begin each workday with prayer, seeking God's wisdom and discernment in decision-making and direction for your career path.

3) **Remain Faithful in Your Work** - Dedicate yourself to excellence and integrity in your professional responsibilities, viewing your work as an opportunity to glorify God. Colossians 3:23-24 encourages, "Whatever you do, work at it with all your heart, as working for the Lord."

4) **Practice Patience** - Embrace seasons of waiting or uncertainty with patience, knowing that God is working behind the scenes for your good and His purpose. Psalm 37:7 advises, "Be still before the Lord and wait patiently for him."

5) **Practice Gratitude** - Develop a heart of gratitude for the opportunities and blessings in your current job, recognizing that every experience contributes to your growth and development. 1 Thessalonians 5:18 encourages, "Give thanks in all circumstances; for this is God's will for you in Christ Jesus."

6) **Seek out Positive Mentors** - Surround yourself with wise counselors and mentors who can offer godly advice and perspective on your career decisions and challenges. Proverbs 15:22 states, "Plans fail for lack of counsel, but with many advisers they succeed."

7) **Let Go of Anxiety** - Release anxiety and worries about the future into God's hands, trusting that He holds your career journey in His sovereign care. Philippians 4:6-7 advises, "Do not be anxious about anything, but in every situation, by prayer and petition, with thanksgiving, present your requests to God." Celebrate your co-workers' success as though they were your own.

8) **Embrace Divine Timing** - Embrace the understanding that God's timing is perfect and often differs from our own expectations. Ecclesiastes 3:11 reminds us, "He has made everything beautiful in its time."

By applying these principles, you can deepen your trust in God's timing at work, fostering a sense of peace, purpose, and confidence as you navigate your professional journey with faith and obedience to His will.

"Success is not a destination, it's a journey." - **Zig Ziglar**

Chapter Eight - Key Takeaways:

1) Understand that delays and setbacks only strengthen your faith and character, preparing you for greater responsibilities and opportunities that are coming your way.

2) Do the right thing, the right way, at the right time, all the time. Build a reputation of excellence.

3) Priorities matter - God, family and work.

Motivational Songs:

1) "God Favored Me" - Hezekiah Walker, The Love Fellowship Choir

2) "No Longer Slaves" - Zach Williams

3) "Won't He Do It" - Koryn Hawthorne

4) "God Did It" - Mervin Mayo

Scripture References:

1) Colossians 3:23-25

2) 1 Thessalonians 5:18

3) Psalm 37:7

4) Romans 8:28

Motivational Quotes-

"The ability to discipline yourself to delay gratification in the short term in order to enjoy greater rewards in the long term is the indispensable prerequisite for success." - **Max Maltz**

A Prayer on "Trusting God's Timing at Work"

Dear Heavenly Father

I lift up my work life to You, recognizing Your dominion over every aspect of it. Grant me the faith and trust to believe in Your perfect timing, knowing that Your plans for me are good and purposeful. Help me to wait patiently for Your blessings, understanding that Your timing is always right.

Lord, create in me a spirit of honesty and integrity in all my dealings at work. May I honor You with my words and actions, seeking to glorify You in every task and interaction. Grant me the strength to persevere through challenges, trusting in Your provision and guidance.

Father, instill resilience in my heart and mind, that I may bounce back from setbacks and disappointments with renewed faith and determination. Help me to rely on Your strength and wisdom, rather than my own understanding.

Thank You, Lord, for Your faithfulness and grace that sustain me in my work. May Your peace reign in my heart, and Your joy be my strength as I trust in Your timing and follow Your leading.

In the precious name of Jesus- Amen

CHAPTER NOTES

SEED, TIME AND HARVEST

When You Make The Investment,
You Can Change The World

This has to be one of my favorite chapters in the book. Writing this chapter has allowed me to reflect on how my parents, grandparents, teachers, and so many other caring people around me have shaped my life. This chapter will allow you to put together the entire framework of how you and I can be a blessing in the lives of so many people around the world. It shows how we can bless people through the giving of our time, talents, kindness, money and so many other things. It shows that at any time in our lives, we can have an impact on the seeds we sow and how we manage our time to reap a bountiful harvest.

In the biblical context, the principle of seed, time and harvest embodies a profound spiritual and practical truth about sowing and reaping, both in agriculture and in the realm of spiritual and moral consequences. This principle, often referred to as the law of sowing and reaping, underscores the idea that what we sow (plant or invest) will eventually be reaped (harvested or received) in due time, whether in terms of blessings or consequences.

The concept of **seed** in the Bible represents that which is sown or planted. It can refer to physical seeds planted in the ground for agricultural purposes, but also metaphorically to actions, words, intentions, or resources that are invested or given with the expectation of a future return.

- Sow in good faith

- Sow with a good attitude

- Sow with expectations

- Sow with anticipation

- Sow without always expecting a return

In Luke 8:11, Jesus explains the parable of the Sower, where the seed represents the word of God that is sown into various types of soil (representing people's hearts). This emphasizes the importance of what is sown spiritually – whether it be the gospel, kindness, generosity, or other virtues – will produce fruit in people's lives according to how they receive and nurture it.

Time, in the biblical context, signifies the period between sowing and reaping – a season of waiting, growth, and maturation. Ecclesiastes 3:1 reminds us that "To everything there is a season, a time for every purpose under heaven," emphasizing the divine timing and order in the process of sowing and reaping.

- Time is patience

- Time is discipline

- Time is commitment

- Time is character

- Time is confidence

- Time is preparation

- Time is sacrifice

- Time is growth

- Time is putting in the work

Patience and perseverance during this period are crucial. Galatians 6:9 encourages believers, "Let us not become weary in doing good, for at the proper time we will reap a harvest if we do not give up." This verse underscores the importance of continuing to sow good seeds and trusting in God's timing for the harvest.

Finally, the **harvest** represents the culmination of the sowing process – the time when the fruits of labor, whether physical or spiritual, are gathered. It symbolizes the manifestation of blessings, rewards, or consequences that result from what was sown.

"No one has ever become poor by giving." – **Anne Frank**

Growing up, I would often listen to our pastor at our local church minister on the topic of seed, time and harvest. Me, being a young child, I didn't truly understand the magnitude of the message. I assumed that it always referred to me or my parents having to give more money in the little offering tray that they passed around or the tithing box that sat at the front of the church for those who were obedient enough to faithfully give 10% of their financial earnings. The message would always somehow end up on the topic of giving money.

My parents would always give each of us money to place in the offering tray. I can't lie, sometimes it was tempting to hold on to a few quarters or an occasional dollar bill or two. Fortunately, at an early age I had the discipline and integrity to give everything to God. Besides, I didn't want to get in trouble with my mom or dad either. Trust me, my parents believed in the infamous "spare the rod spoil the child" verse. (Paraphrased - Proverbs 13:24) ... I think they read that particular verse every day, twice a day... Just kidding!

Back then my parents may not have always had the money to pay their full 10% tithes but they would always give from what they had. Ironically when it was time for the tithes to be collected, the participating members would all gather at the front of the church and the pastor would say a special prayer over their offerings. Each would then place their tithing envelope inside of the tithing box and then return to their seats. Then the regular offering would be collected. I dreamt of one day being bold enough to be able to stand with the tithers in their full obedience in their financial commitment to God. This actually taught me to always strive to at least give 10% of my total earnings diligently.

Later on in my adulthood, I realized that it was about so much more than just money. God looks at your heart and your willingness to be obedient. This message has such a profound meaning and impact on so many people that enter your sphere of influence. Let's dive into additional meanings of this phrase, seed, time and harvest.

I remember listening to a story from legendary motivational speaker and my personal mentor Mr. Les Brown. In his speech he talked about the growth of a Chinese bamboo tree.

Here is a paraphrased illustration of how Les Brown might frame the story:

Imagine planting a Chinese bamboo seed and watering it diligently every day. Despite your efforts, nothing seems to happen in the first year. You continue to water and nurture the seed, yet after the second year, there's still no visible growth above the ground. You might start doubting if anything will ever come of your efforts.

But you persist. For three, four, even five years, you continue to water and care for the seed, with no sign of progress. Some might give up, thinking it's futile. Yet, you keep going.

Then, something miraculous happens. In the fifth year, the bamboo seed suddenly sprouts and shoots up over 80 feet in just a few weeks. What seemed like no progress for years was actually a time of underground growth – developing a strong root system to support the rapid growth that followed.

The lesson of the Chinese bamboo tree is about perseverance. It teaches us that sometimes our efforts may not always yield immediate results, but with patience, consistency, and faith in the process, incredible growth can occur when the time is right. Just as with the bamboo tree, our dreams and goals require nurturing, persistence, and unwavering belief in their eventual fruition.

So often we fail to realize that we possess the power to be a blessing in people's lives. So often our words can serve as the water in Les Brown's metaphoric example. Let me explain.

"You never know when a moment and a few sincere words can have an impact on a life." **Zig Ziglar**

Often God, or even people, plant seeds of hope and prosperity in children and adults. That seed continues to be nurtured by acts of kindness, words of encouragement and various acts that fosters growth and development.

In chapter one, I explained how one day my dad planted seeds of hope and prosperity in me, by telling me how much he loved me and believed in me. He explained to me that he wanted me to one day be better than he was. Well fast forward, six months from that conversation. I remember one of my middle school teachers watering those very seeds. She would often tell me that she was so proud of me and my speaking abilities. She would often say, "Little Jones, you are such a great orator." Honesty at the time, I had no clue what the word orator meant but I took it in stride and assumed that it was something good and positive.

I will never forget how she impacted my life. She invited her husband to sit in on one of my speeches that I presented in her class. He took time from his busy schedule to sit in on my presentation. He was very impressed and I was so excited and grateful for his kind words and support. He would often see my mom and dad around town and speak so highly of me and how I carried myself and my professionalism at such a very young age. Their words of encouragement would forever change my life, for they were watering the seeds of greatness that were planted inside of me.

During my childhood and adolescence, I struggled with reading comprehension. Often I would have to read things several times to completely understand the information. I would often misspell or mispronounce words without realizing it. I learned to always go back and proofread my assignments.

I guess it was in high school and in college that I realized that I potentially had a learning disorder and that I would always have to work harder than everyone else. I had to put in the extra work, I had to be overly committed. I never gave up on myself or my goals and dreams. I would always use my parents' words of encouragement along with my teacher and her husband's wonderful words of support and comfort to maintain my perseverance and determination.

"Sometimes you don't realize your own strength until you come face to face with your greatest weakness." - **Susan Gale**

Then, something amazing happened in my life. I had started my college journey majoring in Computer Science. During this time, I met my then girlfriend and now wife, who was also a Computer Science major and we started dating. Ironically, soon after, I began to realize that I no longer had a passion for Computer Science. So, I changed my major to Business Administration with a concentration in Marketing. I loved the business minded environment. The transition was energetic and refreshing. The core classes that really piqued my interest were Marketing Analytics, Organizational Behavior, Business Ethics and Law, and finally Strategic Management. These classes along with Statistical Analysis and Professional Development, shaped the evolution of my career in upper management.

I was working as a part time supervisor at UPS, this allowed me to gain first-hand knowledge in a real life working environment and classroom knowledge at the same time. I began to flourish at work after partnering with my mentor, Mr. Craft, who took me under his wing and helped me to develop my management style. I also began to flourish in the classroom under the guidance of a very strict professor, Dr Agaro. Understanding the power of statistical analysis, process flow and logical thinking accelerated my classroom and professional growth. He would often make time for one-on-one sessions with me to answer questions and discuss strategies and theories.

I was then sought out for my ability to analyze data and to formulate practical solutions to very complicated classroom cases as well as actual work group areas that functioned with difficulties. I was able to present the solutions in a very professional manner in a classroom setting as well as a business world setting. It didn't matter if I was in front of a college professor or in front of a Regional District Manager at work.

For some reason or another, God has always allowed me to speak with confidence and boldness, even at a very young age, and despite life's challenges. Unbeknownst to my parents and to all of my teachers, my reading and comprehension deficiencies were overshadowed by God's favor and redemptive power in my life.

Seed, time and harvest illustrates the power of God but it also illustrates the power of words and actions during your growth (time) process.

Proverbs 18:21 says ,"Life and death are in the power of the tongue." So many of us are being blessed today from the prayers of our parents, grandparents, spouses, children, family members and so many others that we have met in our various interactions.

We should always be aware of what we say, to whom we say it, and how we say it.

Always remember, just because you have deficiencies in one area of your life, doesn't mean that you won't have strengths in other areas of your life. It may mean that you have to jump a little higher to get over obstacles or hurdles in your way on your journey, but the extra effort only makes your legs (body) and mind stronger.

Don't get caught up on the fact that you have deficiencies or closed doors in your life. Often God will provide you with greater strengths in other areas of your life or provide other opportunities for you in the form of other doors being opened. Quite often the open door could be right next to the closed door, but if you are not careful, you will never notice it because you are still distracted by your deficiency or your closed door.

The biblical reference of seed, time and harvest is masterfully demonstrated in the story of King David.

David's story in the Bible, particularly his journey from shepherd boy to King of Israel, exemplifies the principle of seed, time and harvest in profound ways. From his humble beginnings tending sheep in Bethlehem to his anointing as king by the prophet Samuel, David's life was marked by moments of sowing seeds of faith, courage, and obedience, which eventually yielded a bountiful harvest of blessings and fulfillment of God's promises.

David's journey began with a simple act of obedience and faith when he was anointed by Samuel as the future King of Israel, despite being the youngest and least likely candidate in his family. This initial seed of divine purpose planted in David's heart would grow and shape his destiny in remarkable ways. It was not an instant transformation but a gradual process of growth, learning, and preparation under God's guidance. David did not grow weary waiting on God's promises and plans for his life. David continued protecting his father's sheep from lions and bears all along the way, strengthening his skill set through his use of primitive weapons.

David's encounter with Goliath, the towering Philistine warrior, is perhaps one of the most iconic demonstrations of seed, time and harvest in his miraculous story. When no one in Israel dared to challenge Goliath, David, armed with faith in God and a slingshot, stepped forward to face the giant. His victory over Goliath was not merely a triumph of physical strength but a manifestation of his unwavering trust in God's power and faithfulness. This courageous act sowed seeds of courage, leadership, and faith that would shape David's reputation as a fearless warrior and leader among his people.

Throughout his life, David faced numerous challenges and setbacks, including persecution from King Saul and personal failures such as his affair with Bathsheba. However, David's humility and repentance before God demonstrated another aspect of seed, time and harvest –

the importance of sowing seeds of repentance and humility, and seeking God's forgiveness. Despite his flaws, David's heart remained steadfast in seeking God's will and trusting in His promises.

David's reign as King of Israel was marked by prosperity, military victories, and the establishment of Jerusalem as the capital city. His commitment and obedience to God's commandments and his passion for worshiping God laid the foundation for Israel's spiritual and national growth. The Psalms, attributed to David, reflect his deep intimacy with God and his reliance on divine guidance in every aspect of his life.

David's story is a powerful testament to the principle of seed, time and harvest. Our actions, choices, and attitudes sow seeds that bear fruit over time. Through obedience, faith, courage, repentance, and unwavering trust in God, David experienced the fulfillment of God's promises and became a model of leadership, faith, and devotion for generations to come. His life teaches us that by sowing seeds of righteousness and trusting in God's timing, we can reap a harvest of blessings, fulfillment, and divine purpose in our own lives.

When you invest your time, talents, kindness, and financial resources, the impact reaches far and wide. Currently, my family and I play active roles at our local church. My son and I serve as ushers while my wife and daughter, serve as greeters and also serve in the children's nursery. Welcoming congregants with warmth and friendly greetings brings me immense joy, knowing that our efforts can sow, or even water, seeds of hope and faith into the lives of so many people.

Beyond setting a welcoming tone on Sundays, our interactions throughout the week continue to nurture seeds planted, fostering faith and encouragement in others. It's a privilege to contribute to such a wonderful church that prioritizes and provides financial support to local community outreach and global ministries. I am confident that my tithes and offerings support the spreading of the gospel of Jesus Christ worldwide.

The seeds that we sow through our giving are a blessing to countless individuals globally. I urge you to embrace a lifestyle of consistent generosity. Gracious in giving your time, talents, kindness, and especially financial contributions. As Acts 20:35 reminds us, "It is more blessed to give than to receive."

Together, let us continue to sow seeds that bring hope, faith, and the transformative power of Jesus Christ to communities near and far.

"No one has ever become poor by giving." - **Anne Frank**

Here are 8 ways to encourage faithfulness in seed, time and harvest:

- **Teaching on Generosity** - Share biblical teachings on generosity, such as Proverbs 11:24-25, which emphasizes that those who give freely will prosper and those who refresh others will themselves be refreshed.

- **Stewardship of Talents** - Encourage believers to use their God-given talents and skills to serve others and further God's kingdom. Matthew 25:14-30 (Parable of the Talents) illustrates the importance of using one's talents wisely and faithfully.

- **Tithes and Offerings** - Teach on the biblical principle of tithing and giving offerings as acts of worship and obedience. Malachi 3:10 encourages bringing the whole tithe into the storehouse, promising blessings and abundance.

- **Supporting the Needy** - Emphasize the biblical mandate to care for the poor, widows, and orphans. Galatians 6:9-10 encourages believers to do good to all people, especially to those who belong to the family of believers.

- **Prayer and Fasting** - Promote spiritual disciplines like prayer and fasting, which align hearts with God's will and open opportunities for Him to work in powerful ways. Isaiah 58:6-11 discusses the blessings of fasting and caring for the needy.

- **Faith and Trust in God's Provision** - Teach on trusting in God's provision and faithfulness. Luke 6:38 encourages giving, promising that the measure you give will be measured to you in return.

- **Lead by Example** - Demonstrate generosity in your own life by actively giving your time, sharing your talents, and contributing financially to causes you believe in. Your actions can inspire others to follow suit.

- **Share Stories of Impact** - Share personal stories or testimonies of how giving has made a positive impact, both in your life and in the lives of others. Highlight the tangible benefits and outcomes that result from generosity.

Always offer words of encouragement to everyone that you meet. Always show kindness, compassion, and patience.

By grounding these teachings in scripture and demonstrating how they apply practically in daily life, individuals can be inspired to sow seeds of faith, generosity, and obedience, leading to a harvest of blessings and spiritual growth.

Promoting the principle of seed, time and harvest, as understood biblically, involves encouraging acts of generosity. By fostering a culture of generosity and providing meaningful opportunities for giving, you can encourage others to sow seeds of kindness, compassion, and support that will yield a harvest of positive impact and fulfillment.

Encouraging giving of time, talent, and finances aligns with the principle of seed, time and harvest, where sowing generously leads to a bountiful return.

"Every adversity, every failure, every heartache carries with it the seed of an equal or greater benefit."- **Napoleon Hill**

Chapter Nine - Key Takeaways:

1) Seed, time and harvest is about so much more than just giving of money, it's about your obedience to God.

2) Always strive to be a blessing to others. Giving of your time, talents, kindness, compassion and finances are one of our key assignments from God.

3) Perseverance teaches us that sometimes our efforts may not always yield immediate results, but with patience, consistency, and faith in the process, incredible growth can occur when the time is right. Never give up.

Motivational Songs:

1) "I Give Myself Away" - William McDowell

2) "Famous For (I Believe) - Tauren Wells

3) "You Deserve It" - JJ. Hairston & Youthful Praise

4) "Promise" - Joe L. Barnes, Naomi Raine - Maverick City Music

Scripture References:

1) Luke 6:38

2) Galatians 6:9-10

3) Proverbs 18:21

4) Matthew 25:14-30

Motivational Quote -

"We make a living by what we get, but we make a life by what we give." - **Winston Churchill**

A Prayer on "Seed, Time and Harvest"

Dear Heavenly Father

We come before You with hearts filled with gratitude for Your faithfulness in our lives. Lord, you plant seeds of hope and promise in our hearts. As we begin this journey of seed, time, and harvest, we trust in Your divine timing and provision.

Lord, we acknowledge that the path to harvest is often filled with challenges and roadblocks. Grant us the strength and resilience to persevere through difficulties, knowing that You are our sustainer and source of strength. Help us to remain steadfast in faith and unwavering in our commitment to Your plan for our lives.

Father, we lift up any deficiencies or obstacles that stand in our way. Whether they be doubts, fears, or setbacks, we surrender them to You, knowing that Your power is made perfect in our weakness. Please provide us with daily strength to overcome any shortcomings that we may have. Give us wisdom to discern Your will and courage to walk boldly in obedience.

Lord, please bless us with patience, and obedience in our financial gifts to you. May our words be used to uplift and encourage one another, providing comfort in the times of discouragement and doubt.

May our efforts be fruitful, Lord, as we sow seeds of love, kindness, and compassion in our relationships and endeavors. May we reap a harvest of blessings and abundance that glorifies Your name.

In the precious name of Jesus- Amen

CHAPTER NOTES

CELEBRATING YOUR TOMORROW TODAY

This is your time to be Great

We are all born with goodness inside of us. We determine if that goodness turns into greatness. We all possess the power to turn our goodness into greatness. So many of us have yet to reach our full potential in life. Oftentimes many of us wallow in our own self-pity and fail to get out of our own way to our predestined path to greatness that God has promised and prepared for us. We have to determine which path we will take. Will we take the path of righteousness and eternal life or will we choose the path of sin and its eternal consequences? Ultimately that decision is up to each one of us. No one else on earth can determine your destiny or establish your legacy but you.

We define our legacy by how we live our lives every day. We determine our eternal legacy by the decisions that we make each day. Every day we have a choice and a chance. We have a choice to do the will of God and a chance to ask for forgiveness when we have missed the mark.

We have to determine if we are going to give up, settle for less than what we deserve or keep pressing forward with purpose and resilience.

I thought long and hard on how to end this final chapter. I wanted to culminate with a decisive ending showing the greatness of God. I truly believe that we should always be gracious and thank God for what we have in our lives and to be faithful in trusting God and holding him accountable to what he has promised us. For he said that he would never leave us nor forsake us.

In the end, I wanted to leave a spiritual example and a worldly example of this book's purpose and transformative power. In chapter 9, the story of king David serves as an excellent example of biblical personal goodness being turned into greatness.

For my worldly examples, I had so many wonderful stories to choose from. I could have chosen seven time Super Bowl winner - NFL superstar Tom Brady with his incredible Super Bowl run and his amazing comeback story from his devastating knee injury, or I could have chosen Bethany Hamilton, a professional surfer who made a remarkable comeback after losing her left arm in a horrific shark attack. Then there were the wonderful stories of the GOAT in Gymnastics - Simone Biles and arguably the GOAT on the basketball court - Kobe Bryant.

What a very difficult decision. In the end I chose all four.

- **Let's start with our superstar <u>surfer</u>.**

Bethany Hamilton's life story embodies resilience, faith, and unwavering determination in the face of adversity. Bethany displayed a natural talent and passion for surfing from a young age. Her journey took a dramatic turn on October 31, 2003, when she experienced a life-changing event that would test her spirit and faith in God like never before.

At just 13 years old, Bethany was attacked by a 14-foot tiger shark while surfing off the coast of Kauai in Hawaii. The attack resulted in the loss of her left arm, a devastating blow to her promising surfing career. Many would have seen this as an insurmountable setback, but Bethany's faith in God and her resilient spirit propelled her forward.

Despite the physical and emotional trauma, Bethany refused to let the shark attack define her or derail her dreams. With the support of her family, friends, and her faith community, she embarked on an inspiring journey of recovery and adaptation. Just one month after the attack, Bethany was back on her surfboard, relearning how to surf with one arm. Her determination to pursue her passion for surfing was a testament to her courageous spirit and unwavering faith in God.

Romans 8:18 - "I consider that our present sufferings are not worth comparing with the glory that will be revealed in us."

Bethany's comeback story captured the hearts of people around the world, inspiring millions with her courage and resilience. In 2004, she won the National Scholastic Surfing Association (NSSA) National Surfing Championship, proving that her surfing abilities were stronger than ever. Her perseverance and positive attitude earned her the nickname "Soul Surfer," which later became the title of her autobiography and a feature film based on her life. Bethany is currently married and has 4 amazing children.

Throughout her journey, Bethany has been vocal about the role of her faith in guiding her through her personal challenges. She credits her relationship with God for giving her strength, hope, and a sense of purpose far beyond surfing. Bethany has used her platform to inspire others by speaking at events, sharing her story in interviews, and advocating for causes that she pursues with relentless passion.

In addition to her surfing career, Bethany has become a motivational speaker, author, and philanthropist. She founded the non-profit organization, "Friends of Bethany Hamilton," which supports shark attack survivors and amputees, as well as providing scholarships and community outreach programs.

Bethany Hamilton's resilience and faith continue to inspire people of all ages and backgrounds. Her story is a powerful testimony that will continue to remind the world that with determination, courage, and unwavering faith in God, we can overcome even the most daunting challenges life throws our way.

Bethany's journey is not just about surfing, it's about embracing life's obstacles as opportunities for growth and using adversity to inspire positive change in the world. It's about going through a storm of life and coming out even stronger and wiser.

Bethany's story profoundly embodies the essence of this book. She never gave up, despite unimaginable challenges. She never lost faith in God nor did she ever lose faith in herself or her abilities. The shark may have taken away her arm, but God replaced it with courage and perseverance. How many of us would have even had the courage to get back into the water?

"I think a hero is an ordinary individual who finds strength to persevere and endure in spite of overwhelming obstacles." -

Christopher Reeve

– Now let's speak the language of Football

Tom Brady's athletic journey started from modest beginnings. Despite not being highly recruited initially, Tom's relentless work ethic and dedication earned him a spot at the University of Michigan, where he played college football under coach Lloyd Carr.

Tom's professional career began in 2000 when he was drafted by the New England Patriots in the sixth round of the NFL Draft, an unheralded position for a quarterback who would later achieve such greatness. His early years in the NFL were marked by challenges and setbacks, including being the backup quarterback for his first season. However, Tom's resilience and faith in his abilities allowed him to persevere through adversity.

Tom waited patiently, learned from every opportunity and constantly put in the mental and physical hard work to prepare himself for his harvest on the football field.

In 2001, Tom took over as the starting quarterback for the Patriots after an injury to Drew Bledsoe, the starting quarterback. Against all odds, he led the team to a victory in Super Bowl XXXVI, earning the first of his many championships. This victory marked the beginning of Tom's legacy as a clutch performer in critical moments, earning him the nickname "The Comeback Kid" for his ability to lead his team to victory from seemingly impossible situations.

Throughout his career, Tom has been vocal about the role of faith in his life. He has credited his success to God's guidance and has spoken openly about the importance of prayer and spirituality in his daily routine.

Tom's faith has provided him with a sense of purpose and perspective, allowing him to maintain humility in the face of success and resilience in times of adversity. Tom's faith was tested as he suffered a season ending knee injury in 2008, in which he tore his ACL and his NCL. Tom managed to bounce back from his injury and win 4 additional Super Bowl titles after his devastating injury.

Off the field, Tom has been known for his philanthropic efforts and commitment to charitable causes. He has supported numerous initiatives aimed at improving the lives of children and families in need, demonstrating his belief in using his platform for positive impact across the world.

In 2020, Tom signed with the Tampa Bay Buccaneers after spending 20 seasons with the Patriots, a move that many thought would mark the twilight of his career. However, Tom continued to defy expectations, leading the Buccaneers to victory in Super Bowl LV and earning his seventh championship ring at the age of 43, further solidifying his legacy as one of the greatest athletes of all time. Tom Brady's remarkable career is a testament to resilience, determination, and faith in God.

From his humble beginnings to achieving unprecedented success in the NFL, Tom has exemplified the power of perseverance, hard work and dedication. His journey serves as an inspiration to athletes and individuals alike, showcasing the transformative impact of resilience and unwavering faith in God.

Tom's story also embodies the essence of this book. He never stopped believing in himself and most importantly, he maintained his discipline in trusting God's plan for his life. Tom showed remarkable perseverance and patience throughout his career.

"Obstacles don't have to stop you. If you run into a wall, don't turn around and give up. Figure out how to climb it, go through it, or work around it."- **Michael Jordan**

- — **Now let's talk backflips, and balance bars**

Simone Biles faced adversity from early on. She and her siblings were placed in foster care due to her biological mother's struggles with substance abuse. This turbulent start to life could have set the stage for a different trajectory, but Simone's life was forever changed when she was adopted by her maternal grandparents, Ron and Nellie Biles. Their unconditional love and support provided the stability and nurturing environment that Simone needed to flourish.

Simone's journey in gymnastics and her passion for the sport began at a young age, and her natural talent quickly became evident. She rose through the ranks with remarkable speed, showcasing unparalleled skills and defying gravity with her dynamic performances. However, her path to success was not without its challenges. Throughout her career, Simone has faced numerous personal and professional hurdles, including injuries, the pressures of competition, and the scrutiny of being in the public eye.

Philippians 4:13 "I can do all things through Christ who strengthens me."

Despite these challenges, Simone Biles has consistently demonstrated resilience and an unshakeable faith in God. She has openly shared how her faith has been a guiding force in her life, providing her with strength, peace, and a sense of purpose amid the highs and lows of her gymnastics career. Simone's belief in God's plan for her life has helped her navigate difficult times and embrace opportunities for growth and transformation.

Simone's professional accomplishments are nothing short of extraordinary. She has won a record-breaking number of World Championships (25) and Olympic Medals (7), solidifying her status as the most decorated gymnast in history. Her gravity-defying routines and unmatched skills have redefined the sport of gymnastics, inspiring countless young athletes around the world.

Most importantly, beyond her athletic achievements, Simone Biles' legacy is defined by her courage, resilience, and advocacy for mental health awareness.

In 2021, Simone made headlines by courageously withdrawing from several Olympic events to prioritize her mental well-being, sparking a global conversation about the pressures faced by elite athletes and the importance of prioritizing mental health awareness.

Simone has managed to have a historic comeback in her personal life as well as her professional life. Simone was married in April of 2023. In 2024 she competed in her 3rd straight Olympic games in Paris, France. She managed to stun the world at the age of 27, winning an additional (3) gold and (1) silver medals at the Paris Olympic games.

Simone Biles' journey is a powerful testament to the transformative power of resilience, faith, and unwavering determination. Her ability to overcome adversity and thrive in the face of challenges serves as an inspiration to people of all ages and backgrounds.

Simone's legacy will continue to inspire future generations of athletes to pursue their dreams with passion, perseverance, and a steadfast belief in themselves and a higher purpose.

Simone's story profoundly embodies the essence of this book. Unconditional love, conquering the storm and becoming the best version of yourself exemplify Simone Biles' story. She is the definition of resilience, strength and perseverance.

"You don't drown by falling into water, you drown if you stay there."
- **Zig Ziglar**

> – **Now let's step on the <u>basketball court</u>**

Kobe Bryant's life was a testament to resilience, faith, and unwavering dedication, both on and off the basketball court. Kobe displayed extraordinary talent and determination at a very young age. His journey to greatness, however, was not without its share of challenges and setbacks, which he faced with a combination of grit, faith in God, and a commitment to his family and his legacy.

Early in his career, Kobe experienced personal challenges, including public scrutiny and allegations that tested his marriage to his wife, Vanessa Bryant. Despite these difficulties, Kobe demonstrated resilience and a commitment to his family, working through hardships and prioritizing reconciliation and growth. His faith in God provided him with the strength to navigate through his storms by emphasizing the importance of forgiveness, perseverance, and unconditional love.

Even though Kobe made the initial mistake, he didn't let a pattern of infidelity perpetuate his career. He messed up, acknowledged that he was wrong, asked God for forgiveness, asked his family for forgiveness and ultimately forgave himself. He refused to frustrate the goodness of God's grace and mercy. He remained faithful to his wife, to his family and most importantly faithful in his commitment to God.

On the basketball court, Kobe's career was marked by unparalleled success and determination, but also by significant injuries that threatened to derail his path to greatness.

Throughout his 20-year career with the Los Angeles Lakers, Kobe endured numerous injuries, including a torn Achilles tendon and knee problems, which required extensive rehabilitation and perseverance. His ability to bounce back from these setbacks showcased his resilience and unwavering dedication to the game he loved.

Beyond basketball, Kobe prioritized his family, often sharing his deep affection and commitment to his wife, Vanessa, and their daughters, Natalia, Gianna, Bianka, and Capri. He was a loving father who prioritized spending time with his family and nurturing their growth and development. Kobe's dedication to his family reflected his belief in the importance of unconditional love, sacrifice, and support in achieving personal fulfillment and happiness. Kobe's most important titles were "Girl Dad" and "Husband." Kobe prioritized his love for God, his love for his wonderful family and his relentless love for the game of basketball. That's what I admire most about Kobe Bryant.

"You are not defined by your past mistakes, but by your future actions." - **C. Jones**

Kobe's legacy extends far beyond his achievements on the basketball court. He was a philanthropist, entrepreneur, and advocate for youth sports and education through the Kobe and Vanessa Bryant Family Foundation. His commitment to empowering the next generation, coupled with his belief in the importance of hard work, discipline, and resilience, continues to inspire millions around the world.

Tragically, Kobe's life was cut short in January 2020, along with his daughter Gianna and seven others, in a helicopter crash. His passing was met with an outpouring of grief and tributes from around the world, underscoring the profound impact that he had on countless lives through his basketball career, philanthropy, and dedication to his family.

Kobe Bryant's journey was a testament to resilience, faith in God, and a steadfast commitment to family and legacy. His ability to overcome personal and professional challenges with grace, humility and determination continues to inspire generations, reminding us of the importance of perseverance, unconditional love, and trusting in God's plan for our lives. Kobe Bryant's legacy will forever be remembered as a beacon of hope, courage, forgiveness and resilience in the face of adversity.

Kobe's story profoundly embodies the essence of this book. Unconditional Love, Conquering the Storm, Becoming the Best Version of Yourself, and Celebrating Your Tomorrow Today exemplify

Kobe Bryant's' story. He is the definition of the 4-Cs: Christ-like attitude (courage), commitment, confidence and character.

"In spite of discouragement and adversity, those who are happiest seem to have a way of learning from difficult times, becoming stronger, wiser and happier as a result." - **Joseph B. Wirthlin**

Your past doesn't define or determine your future. Greatness comes the moment that you press the reset button after a failure, setback or after a storm in life.

Bethany, Tom, Simone, and Kobe chose to hit the reset button and never looked back. They each turned the goodness inside of themselves into greatness with their courageous attitudes, commitment to excellence, confidence in themselves and their remarkable character.

Seeds of goodness have already been planted inside of each and every one of us. We possess the power to turn them into greatness. Maybe we will never be the 5 time NBA champion, a professional surfer, the GOAT gymnast or the GOAT on the football field, but maybe - just maybe, we will be the great teacher at a high school that refuses to give up on kids with learning disabilities, or the janitor who always speaks to kids in the hallway and tells them that they have greatness in them.

Galatians 6:9 - "Let us not become weary in doing good, for at the proper time we will reap a harvest if we do not give up."

"Do what you can, When you can, While you can." - **C. Jones**

"Be an Inspiration, through your Perspiration before your Expiration."
- **Les Brown**

March 16, 2020, that was one of the saddest days of my life, but it was also one of the happiest days of my life. That infamous date will forever resonate in my mind, for that was the day of my dad's funeral.

As I sat in the audience. I listened to family members, friends and neighbors talk about the wonderful things that my dad had done in his life and how he had impacted their lives.

I began to stare at the front page of the obituary that I held in my hand. I focused on the dates including the dash in between the dates. Then it dawned on me, everything that they were talking about was my dad's dash, his legacy, the things that he would forever be remembered for.

My challenge to you is this:

Start thinking about what your dash looks like?

What legacy are you leaving behind?

We are all writing our legacy today for tomorrow.

Our actions today define our legacy for tomorrow.

What gift or talents do you have that you are not utilizing to the best of your ability?

Zig Ziglar once said – "You are the only person on earth who can use your ability."

Motivational Quote - "You were designed for accomplishment, engineered for success, and endowed with the seeds of greatness."

- Zig Ziglar

Thank God for what you have,
always trusting him for what you need.

This is my story...Be blessed!

Chapter Ten - Key Takeaways:

1) We all possess the power to turn our goodness into Greatness.

2) We define our legacy by how we live our lives every day.

3) With determination, courage, and unwavering faith in God, we can overcome even the most daunting challenges life throws our way.

Motivational Songs:

1) "Jesus Is Love" - Lionel Richie - The Commodores

2) "I Can Only Imagine" - Amy Grant

3) "Praise" - Brandon Lake, Chris Brown & Chandler Moore

4) "There Was Jesus" - Zach Williams & Dolly Parton

Scripture References:

1) 2 Corinthians 4:16-18

2) James 1: 2-4

3) Romans 5: 3-5

4) Isaiah 40:31

Motivational Quotes-

"Aspire to Inspire before you Expire." - **Eugene Bell Jr**.

A Prayer on "Celebrating Your Tomorrow Today"

Unleashing Your Inner Greatness

Dear Heavenly Father,

Thank You for the gift of today and the promise of tomorrow. As I stand at the threshold of each new day, I seek Your guidance and strength to celebrate the potential You have placed within me. Help me to recognize and embrace the greatness You have woven into my being, even before I fully see it manifest.

Lord, grant me the wisdom to appreciate the opportunities and blessings of today while holding on to the hope and vision of what tomorrow holds. Teach me to be fully present in each moment, finding joy and purpose in the journey rather than waiting for future achievements to define my value.

Guide me to tap into the talents and abilities You have bestowed upon me. Lord, please light the path that You have set before me and give me the courage to step forward with faith, knowing that You are with me every step of the way. Help me to overcome self-doubt and to believe in the greatness that lies within, inspired by Your promises and love.

May I use today's gifts and opportunities to honor You, celebrating each step towards the fulfillment of my purpose. Empower me to act with integrity, diligence, and passion, trusting that as I align my actions with Your will, I will see the fruits of my labor and the unfolding of Your divine plan for my life.

Thank You, Lord, for the assurance that every day is a chance to celebrate, grow, and advance towards the future that You have in store for me. May Your grace continue to guide and inspire me as I embrace the journey with love, hope and joy.

In the precious name of Jesus - Amen

CHAPTER NOTES

_____

_____

_____

_____

_____

_____

_____

_____

_____

_____

_____

_____

_____

_____

_____

_____

_____

_____

_____

_____

_____

_____

AUTHOR'S
CONTACT INFORMATION

Social Media Outlets:

Facebook: @Cyris Jones

Instagram: @cyrisjones

Email: cyris@cyrisjones.com

Website: https://cyrisjones.com

AUTHOR BIO

Cyris Joseph Jones was born and raised in Prentiss, a small town in Central Mississippi. The ninth of eleven children, Cyris credits his parents, Madis and Willie Jones, for instilling in him the values of hard work, perseverance, and faith. He earned a Bachelor of Business Administration with a concentration in Marketing from Jackson State University, where his leadership journey began.

Cyris has had an illustrious career spanning over three decades. He started with a major logistics company while attending college, advancing into management, and later spent 20 years in various upper management roles at a leading automotive manufacturing firm in Central Mississippi. After retiring from corporate America in 2023 to care for his mother, Cyris turned his focus to his true passion - motivating others, inspiring change, and helping people grow personally and professionally.

Cyris has been happily married to his wife, Terri Jones, for 26 years. Together, they have two children, Christian and Torri, who continue to be a source of pride and inspiration in his life.

Now an author, motivational speaker, and business consultant, Cyris continues to impact lives. He has been mentored by iconic figures like Les Brown and Dr. Denise Nicholson and is preparing for his TEDx debut as an emerging voice in personal development.

Cyris' debut book, "Thank God for What You Have, Trust God for What You Need", is an inspirational self-help memoir designed to uplift and empower readers to embrace faith, gratitude, and perseverance. Beyond his professional pursuits, Cyris enjoys coaching sports, mentoring, traveling, home improvement projects, and serving as an usher at his church. He resides in Jackson, Mississippi, with his family.